Origami Book Three

Japanese Paper-Folding

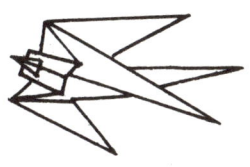

by Florence Sakade

illustrated by Kazuhiko Sono

CHARLES E. TUTTLE COMPANY
Rutland, Vermont   Tokyo, Japan

Representatives

For Continental Europe:
BOXERBOOKS, INC., *Zurich*

For the British Isles:
PRENTICE-HALL INTERNATIONAL, INC., *London*

For Australasia:
PAUL FLESCH & CO., PTY. LTD., *Melbourne*

For Canada:
HURTIG PUBLISHERS, *Edmonton*

*Published by the Charles E. Tuttle Company, Inc.
of Rutland, Vermont & Tokyo, Japan
with editorial offices at
Suido 1-chome, 2-6, Bunkyo-ku, Tokyo, Japan*

©1959 by Charles E. Tuttle Co., Inc.

All rights reserved

Library of Congress Catalog Card No. 57-10685

International Standard Book No. 0-8048-0456-7

*First edition, 1959
Thirty-fifth printing, 1975*

PRINTED IN JAPAN

Table of Contents

	Introduction	4
1.	SPINET	6
2.	CAPS	7
3.	WHALE	8
4.	BIRD	9
5.	SWALLOW	10
6.	TENT	12
7.	JET PLANE	13
8.	FROG	14
9.	PRINCE AND PRINCESS	16
10.	MOTORBOAT	18
11.	PIG	20
12.	CHAIR	21
13.	TABLE	22
14.	SPACE SHIP	24
15.	TREASURE BOX	25
16.	PENGUIN	26
17.	APPLICATIONS OF ORIGAMI	28
	Party Decorations	28
	Boat Race	30
	Mobile	31
	Space Travel	31
	Hunting Game	32

Introduction

THE PLEASURE of creating various objects from square pieces of paper is a fascinating art handed down for generations in the Orient. I am delighted to know that *origami*, this Japanese art of paper-folding, is no longer a favorite hobby only for Japanese but also for both children and adults in foreign lands who have responded so enthusiastically to my first two books on paper-folding. Last Christmas when I visited the U.S. Army Yoyogi Elementary School in Tokyo, I was surprised to find, in Grade 4 classrooms, Christmas trees with no other decorations but *origami* creations from my *Origami: Book One* and *Book Two*.

In response to this encouragement from children, parents, and teachers abroad, I have followed my first two books with this third volume of the series. I am sure that those who are already familiar with my first two books will find that the creations in this third book are just as easy to master as those found in the first two. As in my first two books, here again I have avoided complicated figures and limited myself to those that can be folded even by the beginner. You will find that some of the basic steps are partial repetitions of those found in the previous books. In these cases I have referred to the pages in the earlier books which show these steps, although the directions in this book are sufficient in themselves.

In the second book I introduced finger-play with *origami* objects, and maybe some of you have already found other interesting uses for your favorite creations. In this book I have shown several other ways in which you can use *origami* figures, especially for parties and games with your friends. Besides these, of course, there are many other possibilities for using *origami* figures in three-dimensional effects, such as in backgrounds for plays, sand-table displays, and murals in classrooms. This book gives you some suggestions, but no doubt you can think of still other ways to increase your pleasure, not only in creating the various objects but also in using them.

Solid-color squares of thin paper are best for the beginner to use, but you can later vary your creations by using a wider variety of papers. Wax paper, for example, is excellent for making boats. The beautiful patterns of gift-wrapping papers will add interest to your *origami* figures, particularly those of birds, flowers, and the "Prince" and "Princess." Still other variations can be obtained by using colored cellophane. Delightful two-color effects can be achieved by using two sheets of different-colored paper, folding them simultaneously. After you have acquired enough skill, you can vary the size of the squares you use, so that you will be able to make anything from tiny birds to hats and caps big enough to wear. Perhaps you will even reach such a degree of skill that you can fold a bird from a one-inch square of paper or the wrappings from candies, as Japanese children learn to do in order to show their facility at *origami*.

Undoubtedly those who have already tried their skill are familiar with the necessary points to keep in mind when making these paper-foldings, but for the benefit of those who are just beginning to try their hand, I would like to repeat that:

1. All of the objects are made by folding perfectly square pieces of paper. At first, about four- to six-inch squares are easiest to work with.
2. You must follow the directions step by step; proper shapes can only be obtained through careful, symmetrical foldings.
3. If the figures seem too complicated, practice first by making marks on the corners of your paper to correspond with those in the diagrams.

Origami is, then, the expression of intricate figures through simple folded lines. It is surprising what charming figures can be created through plain geometrical foldings. I hope that this third book, together with the first two, will widen children's experiences in creative enjoyment and, at the same time, teach them the values of color harmony and help them to acquire patience, proper coordination, concentration, and the ability to follow directions.

I am indebted to Messrs. Tokihiko Morikuni, Katsuyo Hayashi, Takayuki Kanai, and Toshio Hayashi for their assistance in the preparation of this book.

FLORENCE SAKADE

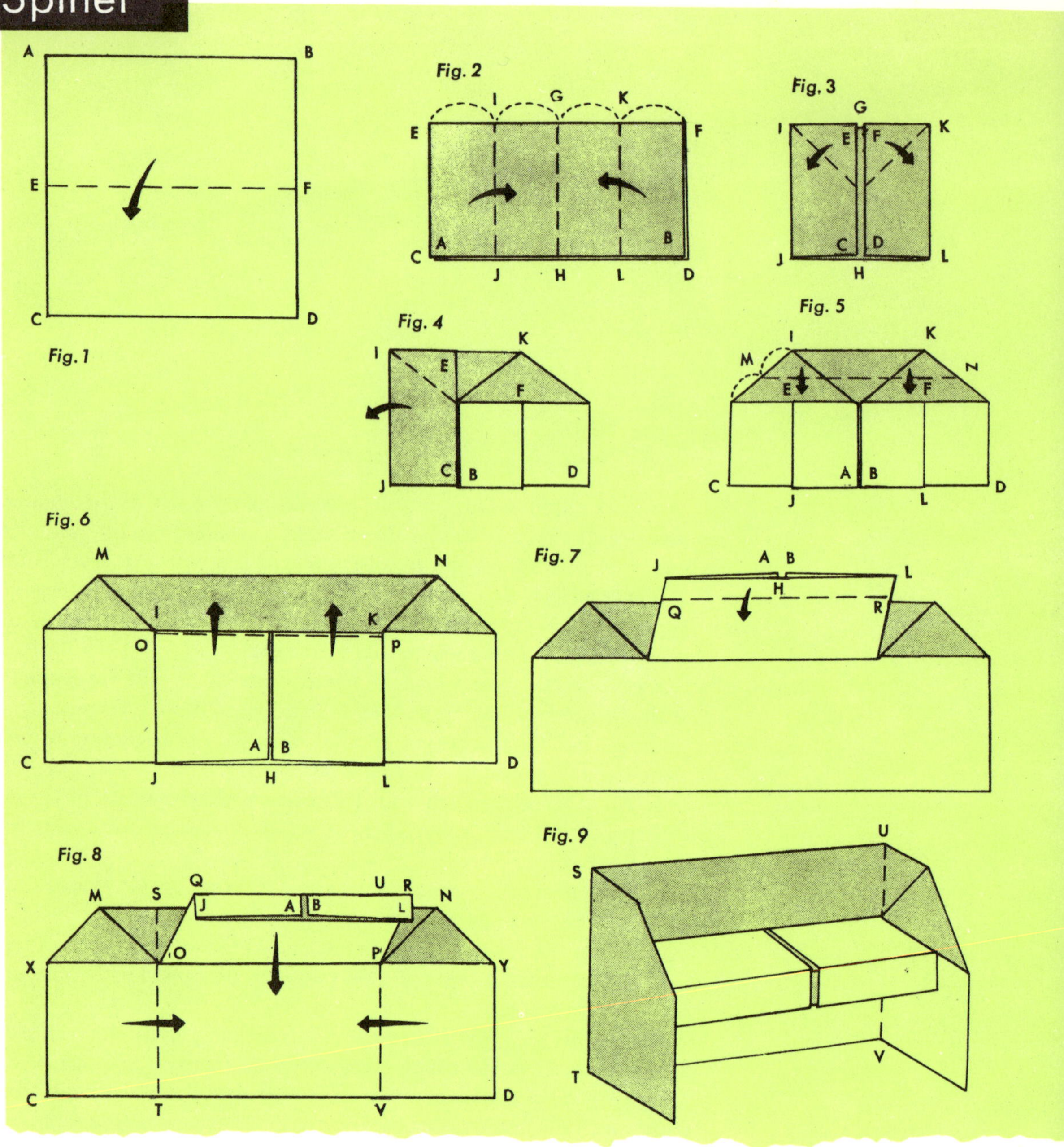

Spinet

1. Fold a square piece of paper along line EF (FIG. 1) so that AB falls on CD (FIG. 2).
2. Fold along IJ and KL (FIG. 2) so that edges AEC and BFD meet at center GH (FIG. 3).
3. Open corner F (FIG. 3) by lifting D toward the right while holding B in place (FIG. 4).
4. Repeat step 3 with corner E (FIGS. 4 & 5).
5. Fold along MN so that IK falls on EF (FIG. 6).
6. To make the keyboard, fold along OP (FIG. 6), bringing JHL forward (FIG. 7) and making OJ and PL right angles to I and K.
7. Fold again at QR (FIG. 7), bringing JABL forward and down and forming right angles at Q and R (FIG. 8).
8. Fold at ST, making XO touch OQ; do the same for UV so that YP touches RP (FIGS. 8 & 9), thus forming right angles at T and V.

Caps

1. To make "Nurse's Cap," repeat steps 1 through 4 in "Spinet" (PAGE 6).
2. Turn paper over and fold along KM and IN (FIG. 6) so that edges OD and PC meet at center (FIG. 7).
3. Fold the top flap along QR; then again at ST; at UV; at WX (FIGS. 7 & 8).
4. Repeat step 4 on the opposite flap and draw a cross to complete (FIG. 9).

---

1. For "Scout Cap" or "Billfold," repeat steps 1 and 2 in "Nurse's Cap" (FIG. 6).
2. Fold the top flap along FN (FIG. 7).
3. Fold again at FE (FIG. 8) so that point N falls on I (FIG. 9).
4. Do the same for the other flap.
   This is a billfold when closed. It can be worn as a Scout or a GI cap and, with the addition of a feather mark, it can be turned into a stewardess's cap.

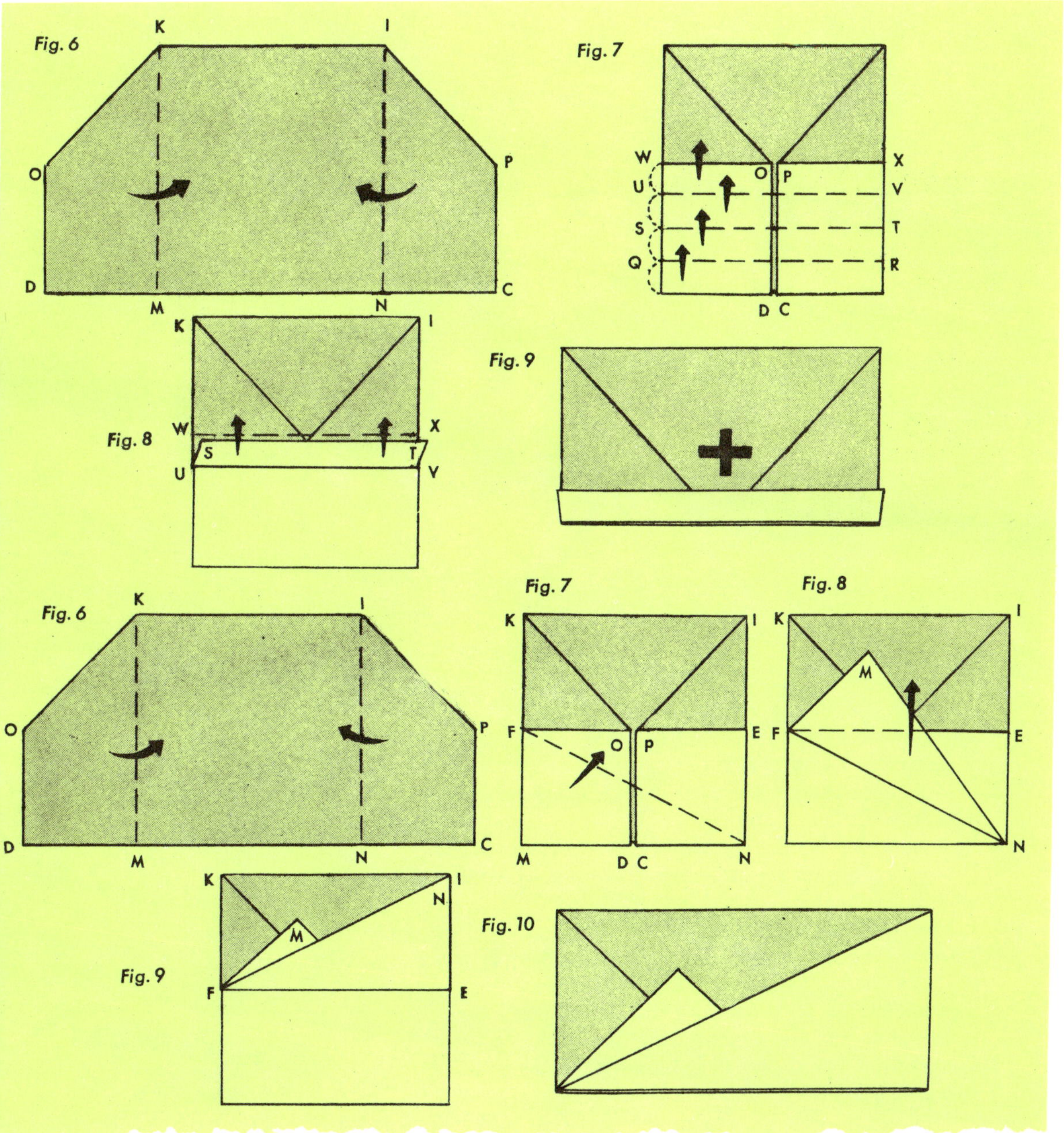

Whale

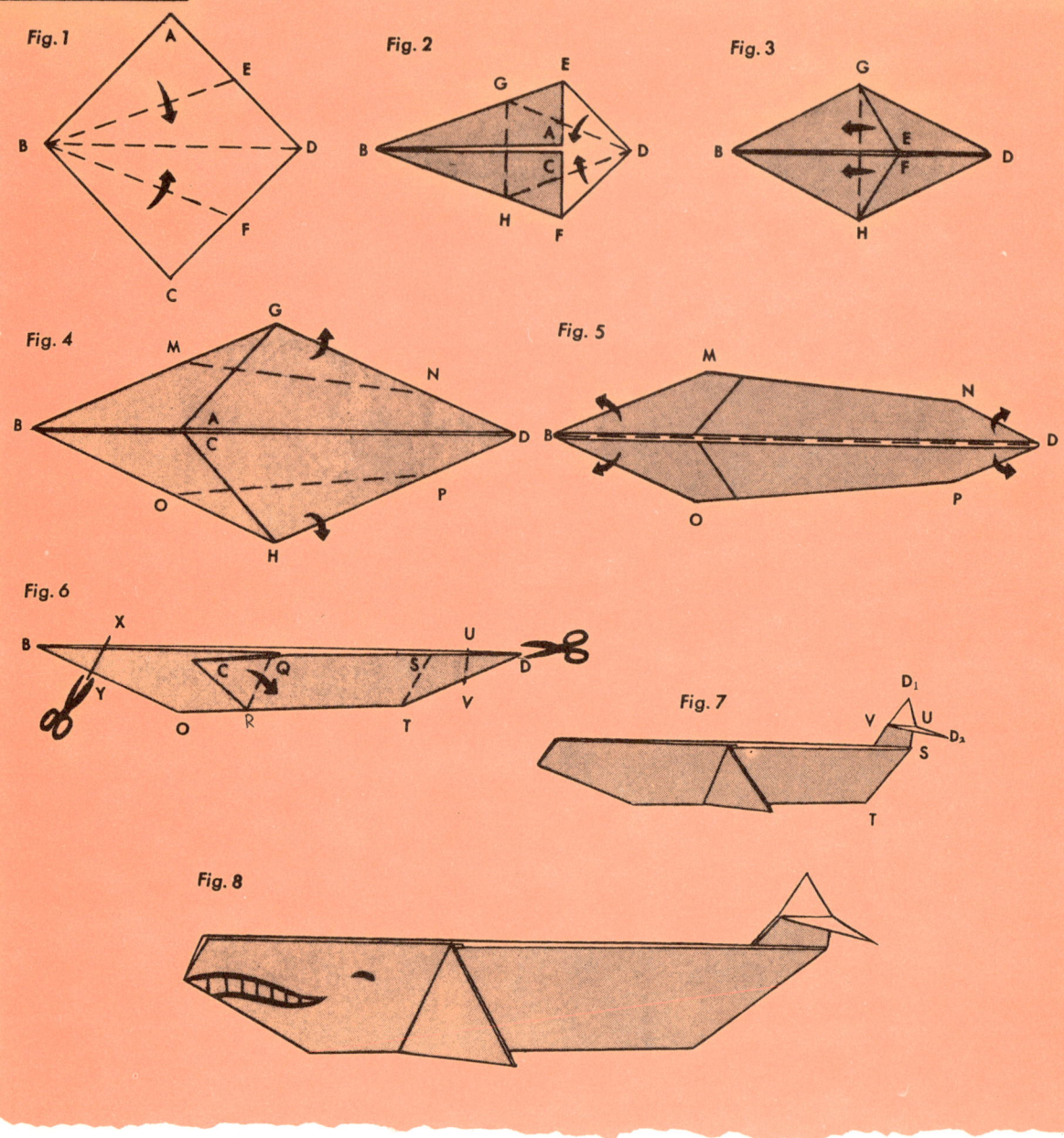

1. Fold a square piece of paper along BE and BF so that edges BA and BC meet at center line BD (FIGS. 1 & 2).
2. Fold along GD and HD (FIG. 2) so that ED and FD meet at center line BD (FIG. 3).
3. Pull out corners A and C so that they meet at center line BD (FIG. 4).
4. Fold back along MN and OP so that G and H meet at center line on the other side (FIG. 5).
5. Fold in half along BD to make the body (FIG. 6).
6. To make the fins, fold at QR, bringing corner C downward and away from the body (FIG. 6). Do the same for the other side.
7. To make the tail, fold back along ST (FIG. 6). Make a slit at UD and open D_1 and D_2 at VU (FIG. 7).
8. Cut off point B at XY (FIG. 6) and draw the mouth and eyes (FIG. 8).

Bird

1. Fold a square piece of paper along AC (FIG. 1) so that corner B falls on corner D (FIG. 2).
2. Fold along EF (FIG. 2), bringing corners B and D to the left (FIG. 3). AE is a little less than one-half of the way down AD (FIG. 2).
3. Fold along GH (FIG. 3), bringing only corner D to the right while keeping B in place (FIG. 4).
4. Fold along BD (FIG. 4) so that edge AE falls on CF (FIG. 5).
5. Fold along IJ at a slant (FIG. 5) or horizontally along XY (FIG. 6) on the top flap of the body. Fold along KE, bringing A to the left (FIGS. 7 & 8).
6. Repeat steps 5 and 6 on the other side.
7. To make the head, crease at LM (FIG. 7) and bring point D down between the flaps (FIG. 8).

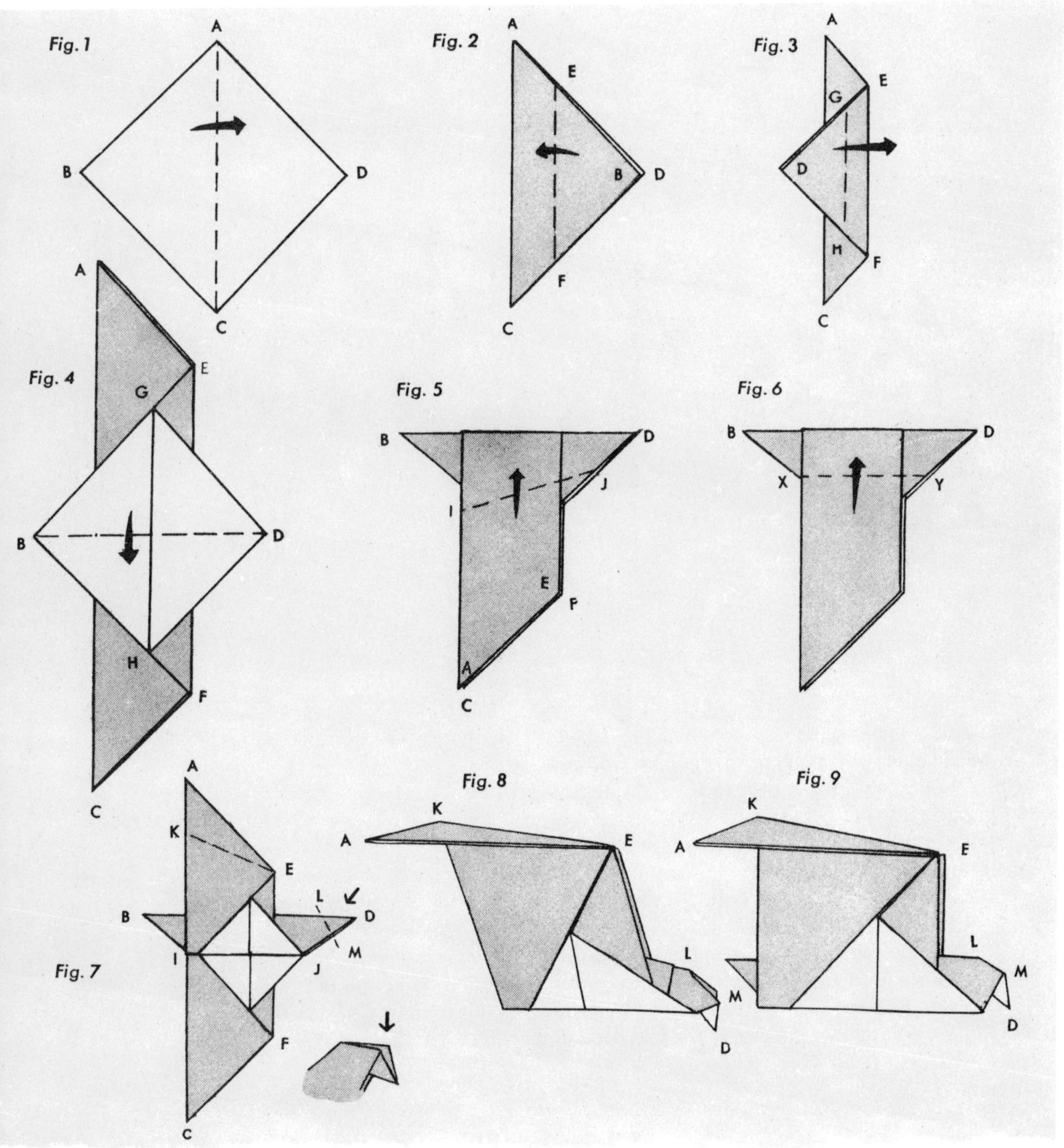

Swallow

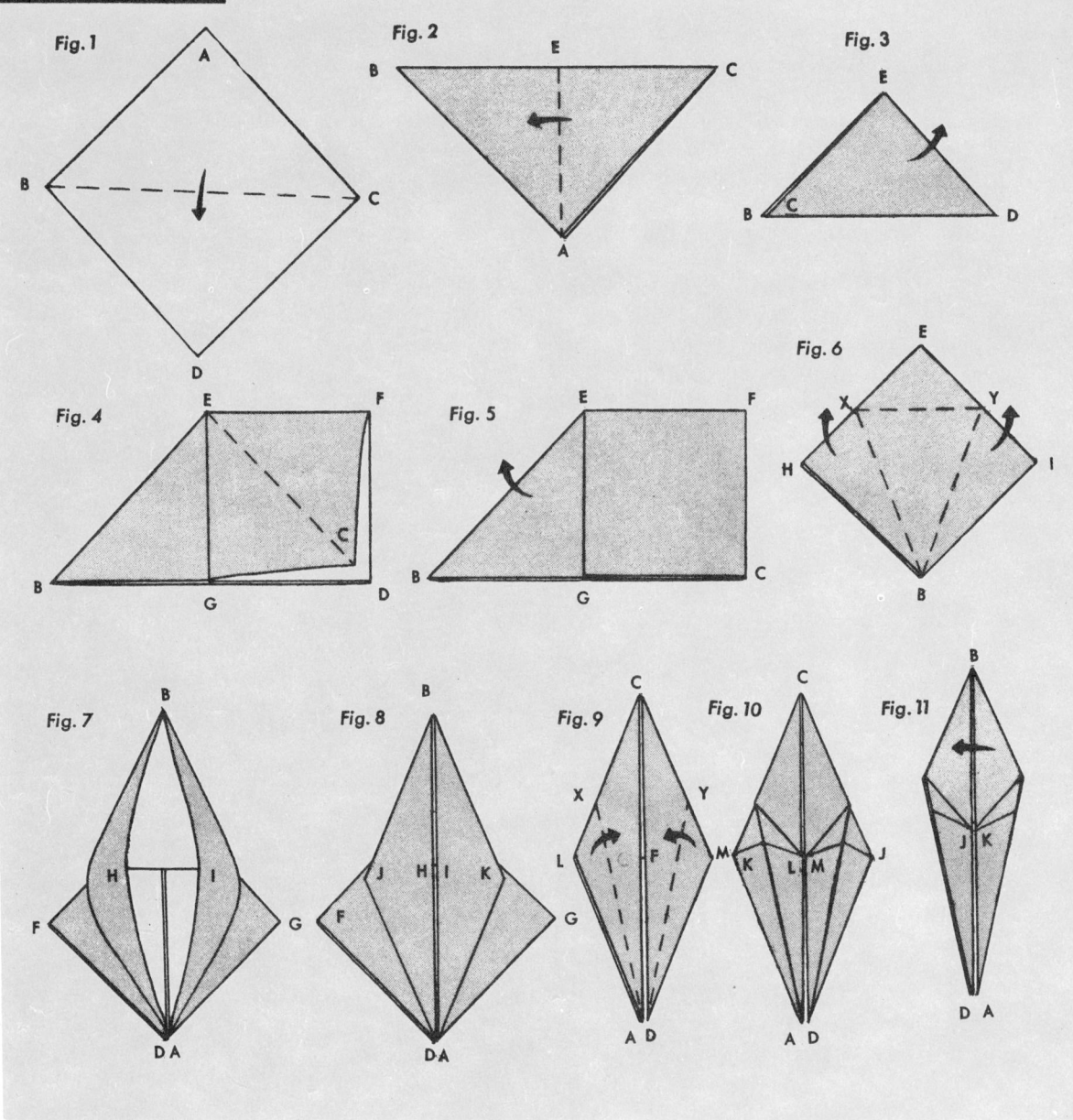

1. Fold a square piece of paper along line BC (FIG. 1) so that corner A falls on corner D (FIG. 2).
2. Fold along EA (FIG. 2) so that point C falls on B (FIG. 3).
3. Open C and bring it over to the right directly above D (FIG. 4). Place C on D and crease EF and EG (FIG. 5).
4. Turn the paper over and repeat step 3 with B (FIGS. 5 & 6).
5. Crease at XB and YB (FIG. 6) so that HB and IB meet at center EB and open.
6. Lift up B and fold at XY (FIG. 6) so that H and I meet at the middle on BD and BA, respectively (FIGS. 7 & 8).
7. Turn the paper over and repeat steps 5 and 6 on the other side (FIG. 9).
8. Fold along XA and YD (FIG. 9) so that L and M meet at center on top of G and F (FIG. 10).
9. Turn the paper over and repeat step 8 on the other side for K and J (FIG. 11).*
10. Take the top flap and fold to the left, making K fall on J (FIG. 11).

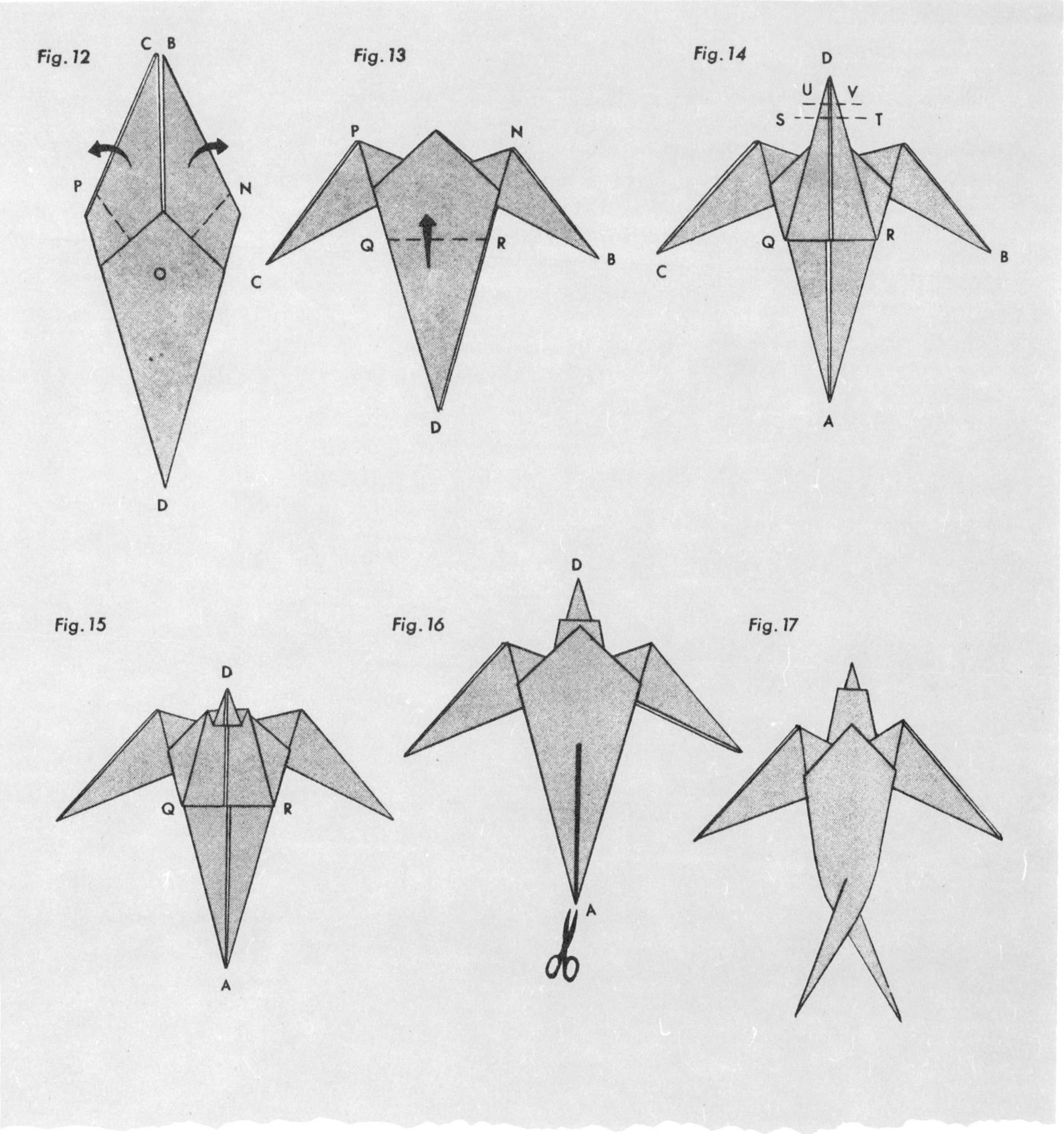

Fig. 12   Fig. 13   Fig. 14

Fig. 15   Fig. 16   Fig. 17

11. Repeat same on the other side, making M fall on L (FIG. 12).
12. To make the wings, bring B down to the right in between the two flaps and fold at ON (FIGS. 12 & 13). Do the same for C, folding at OP (FIG. 13).
13. Lift D to the front and up, folding at QR (FIGS. 13 & 14).
14. To make the head, fold along ST, bringing D forward and down; fold again at UV, making D point upward (FIG. 15).
15. Turn the paper over. Cut one-third of the way up along AD from A (FIG. 16) and make both parts of the tail cross each other (FIG. 17).

* See *Origami: Book One*, p. 30, "Crane," Figs. 1–12, or *Origami: Book Two*, p. 22, "Robin," Figs. 1–9.

Tent

1. Fold a square piece of paper along EF (FIG. 1) so that AB falls on CD (FIG. 2) and crease in the middle at GH.
2. Open corner F (FIG. 2) and bring point F down between B and D so that GF falls on GH (FIG. 3). Crease GB and GD.
3. Turn the paper over and repeat step 3 with E (FIGS. 4 & 5).*
4. Crease along JK, JL, KM, making corners G, C, A meet on E and open (FIG. 5).
5. Lift up E so that it falls on G while corners C and A meet at center (FIG. 6). Fold along ON, OP (FIGS. 7 & 8).
6. Turn the paper over and repeat steps 5 and 6 on the other side.

* See *Origami: Book One*, p. 14, "Flowers," Figs. 1–4, or *Origami: Book Two*, p. 26, "Church," Figs. 1–4.

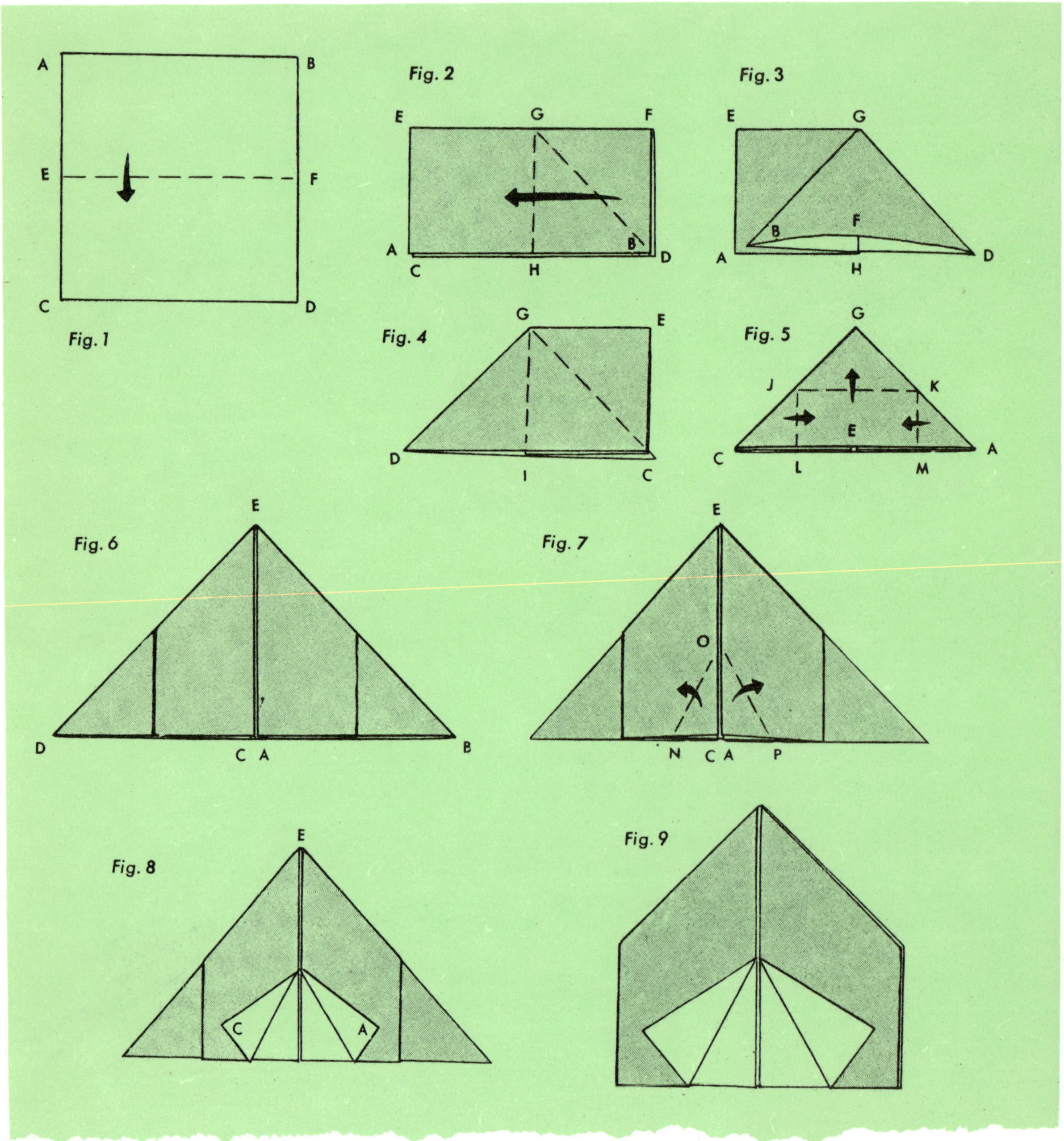

Jet Plane

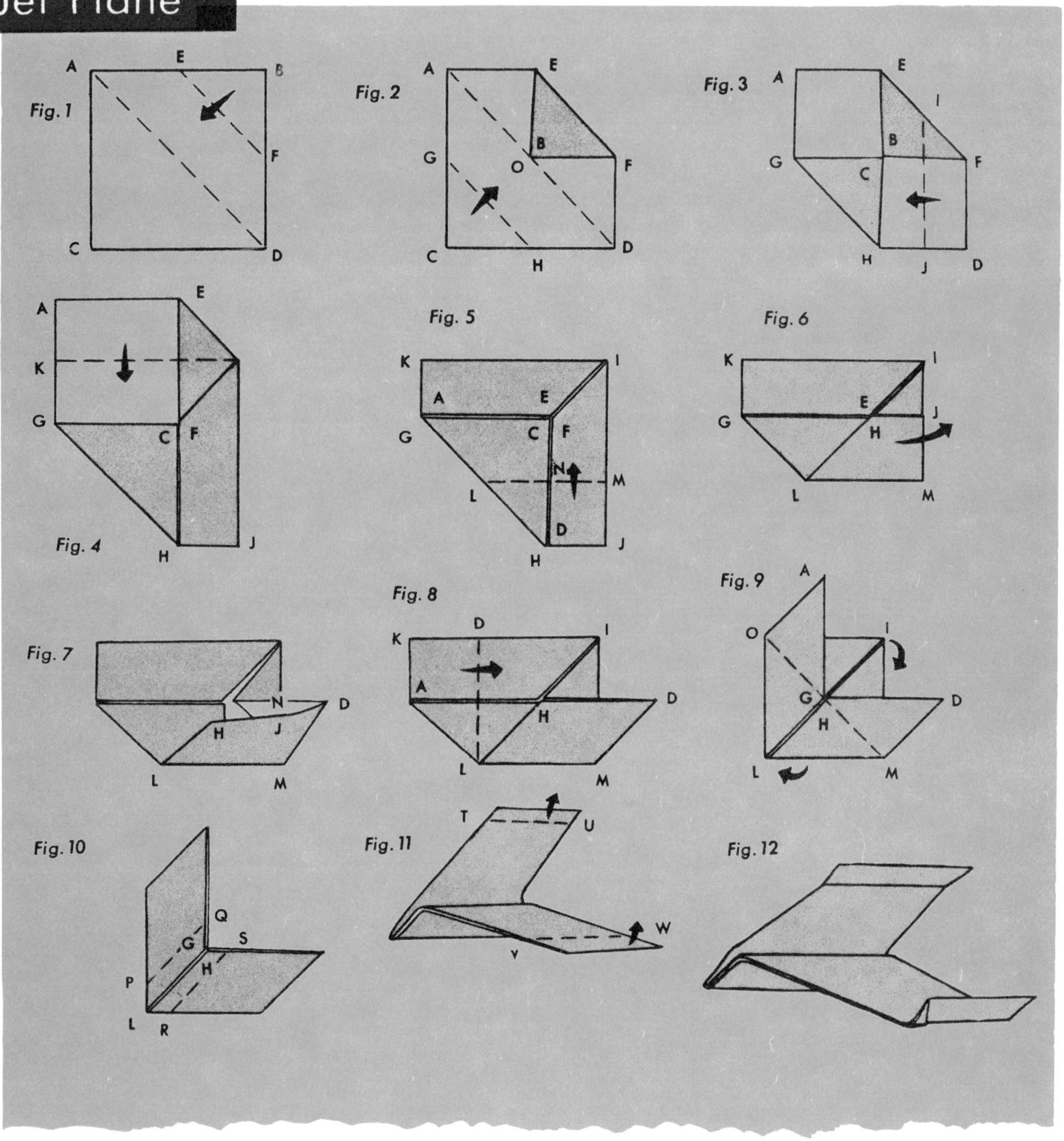

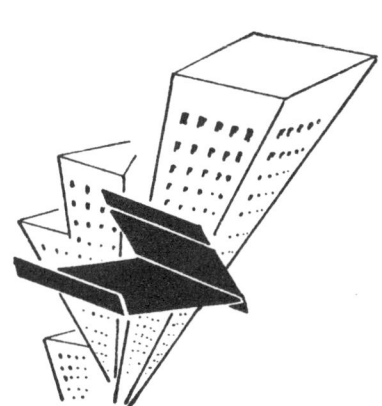

1. Fold a square piece of paper along EF (FIG. 1) so that corner B meets center O (FIG. 2).
2. Fold along GH (FIG. 2) so that corner C meets B at center O (FIG. 3).
3. Fold along IJ (FIG. 3) so that edge FD meets CH (FIG. 4).
4. Fold along KI (FIG. 4) so that edge AE meets GC (FIG. 5).
5. Fold along LNM (FIG. 5) so that D falls on F (FIG. 6).
6. Open corner J, bringing corner D to the right, thus making MJ fall on MN (FIG. 7).
7. Repeat steps 5 and 6 with A (FIGS. 8 & 9).
8. Fold back I along OM so that corner I falls underneath L (FIG. 9).
9. Fold along PQ and RS so that the two sides touch each other (FIG. 10).
10. Fold along TU and VW (FIG. 11) so that the two edges turn up (FIGS. 11 & 12).

Frog

1. Fold a square piece of paper along line BC (FIG. 1) so that corner A falls on corner D (FIG. 2).
2. Fold along EA (FIG. 2) so that point B falls on C (FIG. 3).
3. Open B (FIG. 3) and bring it over to the right, directly above D (FIG. 4). Place B on D and crease EF and EG.
4. Turn the paper over and repeat step 3 with C (FIGS. 4 & 5).
5. Crease at XC and YC (FIG. 6) so that edges HC and IC meet along center line EC and open.
6. Lift up C and fold at XY (FIG. 6) so that H and I meet at the middle on CD and CA, respectively (FIGS. 7 & 8).
7. Turn the paper over and repeat steps 5 and 6 (FIG. 9).*
8. Fold top flap to the left (FIG. 10) so that J falls on top of K.
9. Turn over and repeat step 8 on the other side (FIG. 10) and turn figure upside down (FIG. 11).
10. To make hind legs, lift B back between the flaps and to the right, and C to the left (FIGS. 12 & 13).

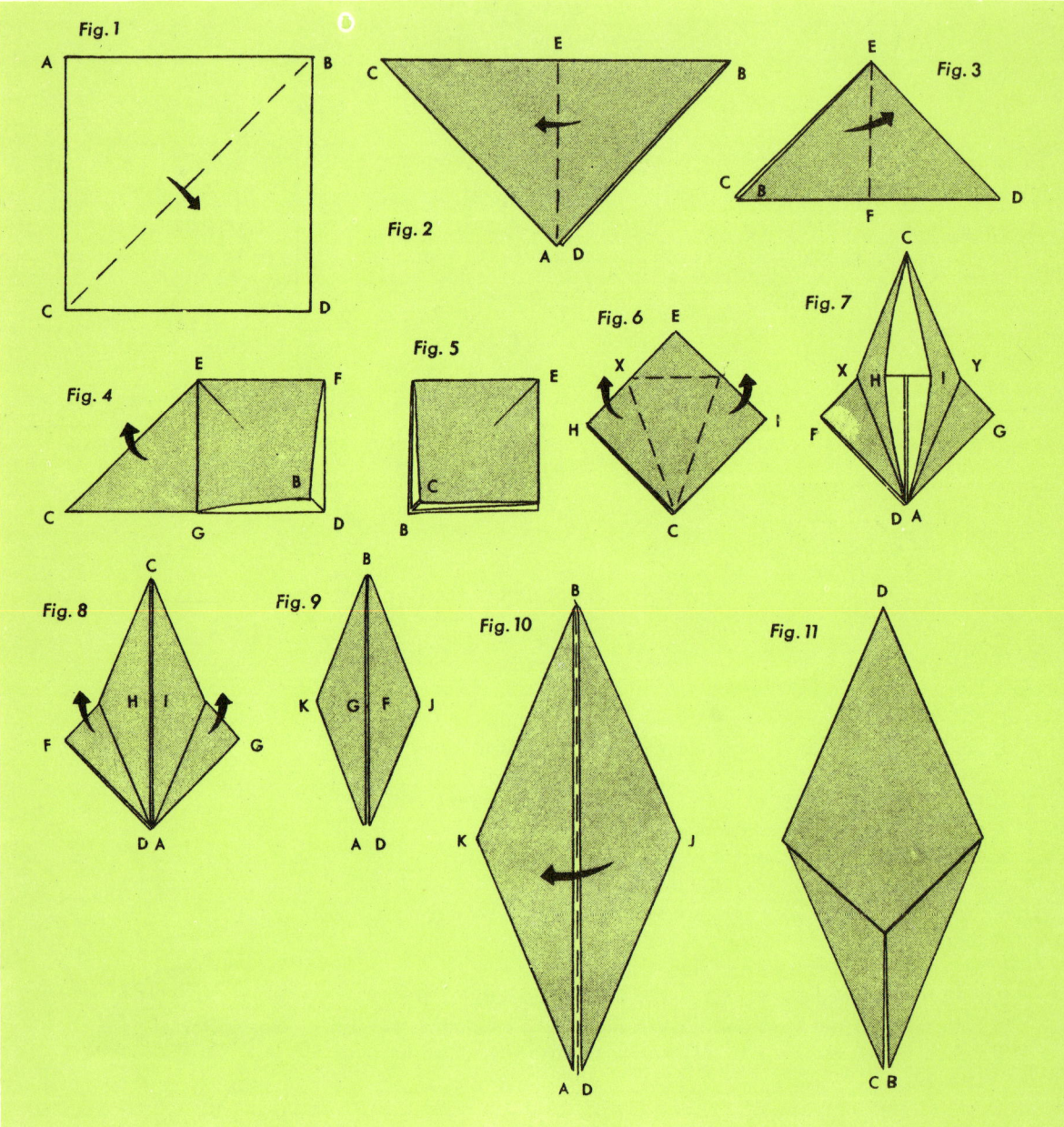

11. Fold along LM and NO so that B and C are bent forward again on both sides (FIGS. 13 & 14).
12. Cut the top flap only from D toward E about two-thirds of the way down the body flap (FIG. 13).
13. Fold along PQ and PR (FIG. 14) so that corners D₁ and D₂ stretch out on both sides of the body flap (FIG. 15).
14. Fold ST and UV (FIG. 15), making the two points D₁ and D₂ face upward towards A (FIG. 16).
15. Fold along WZ so that corner A comes down to the front (FIG. 16). Turn over (FIG. 17).

* See *Origami: Book One*, p. 30, "Crane," Figs. 1–10, or *Origami: Book Two*, p. 22, "Robin," Figs. 1–9.

Fig. 12

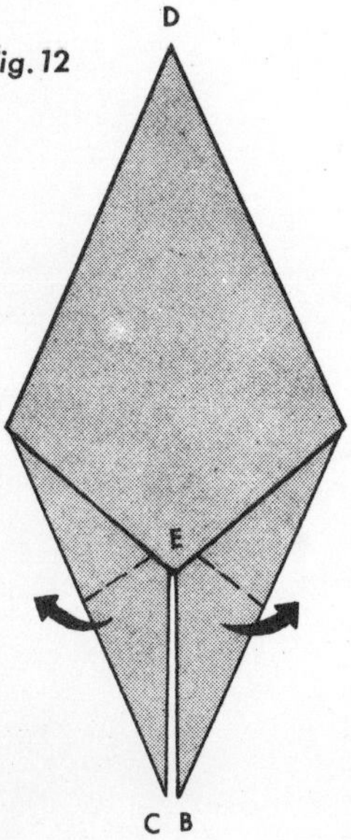

Fig. 13

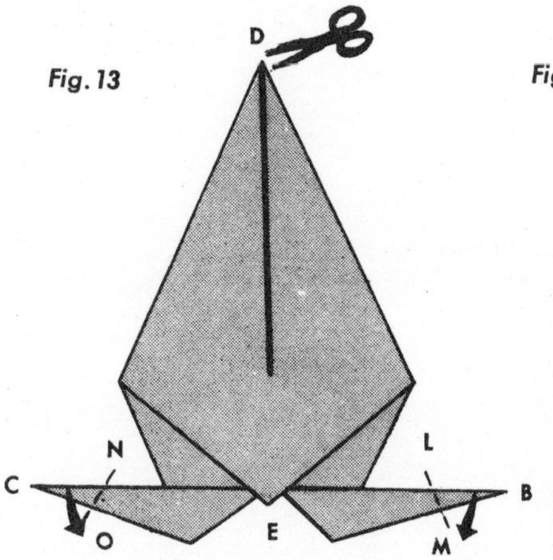

Fig. 14

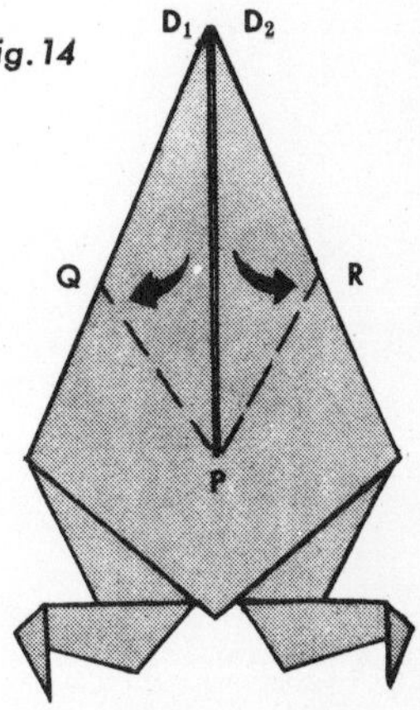

Fig. 15

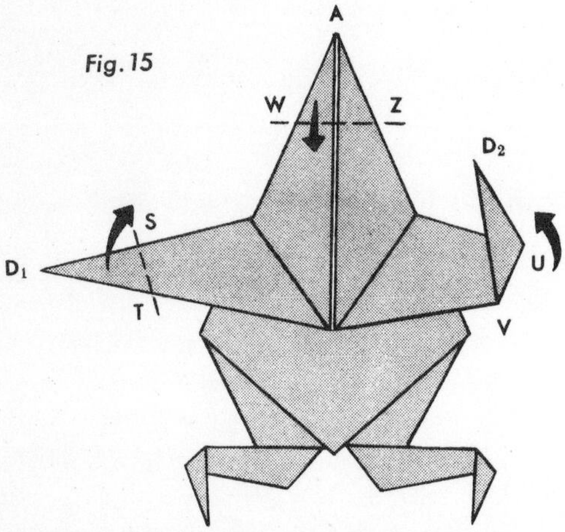

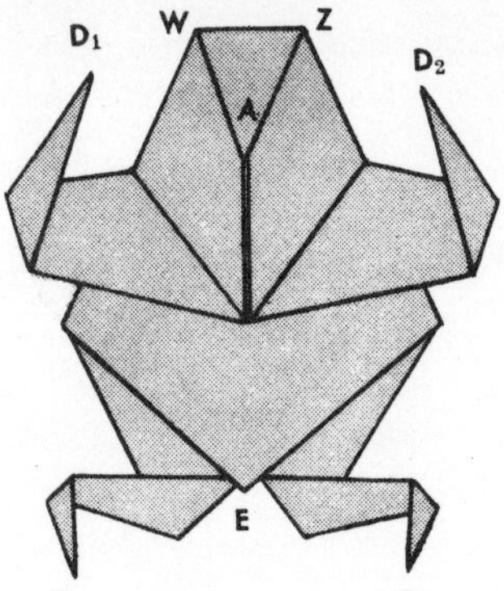

Fig. 16

Fig. 17

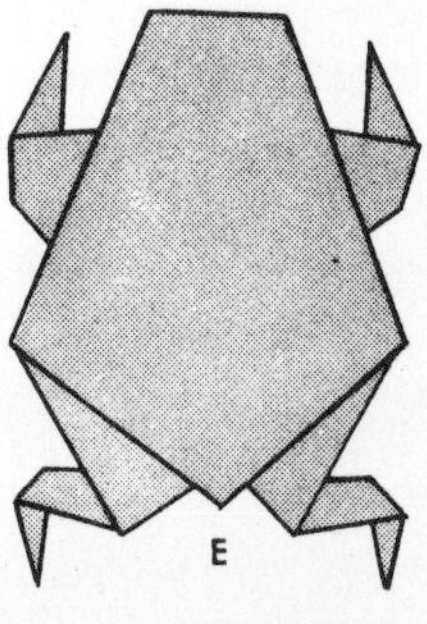

Make the frog move by tapping at E with your forefinger. You can also make several frogs and have a frog race with your friends and see whose frog wins the race.

Prince and Princess

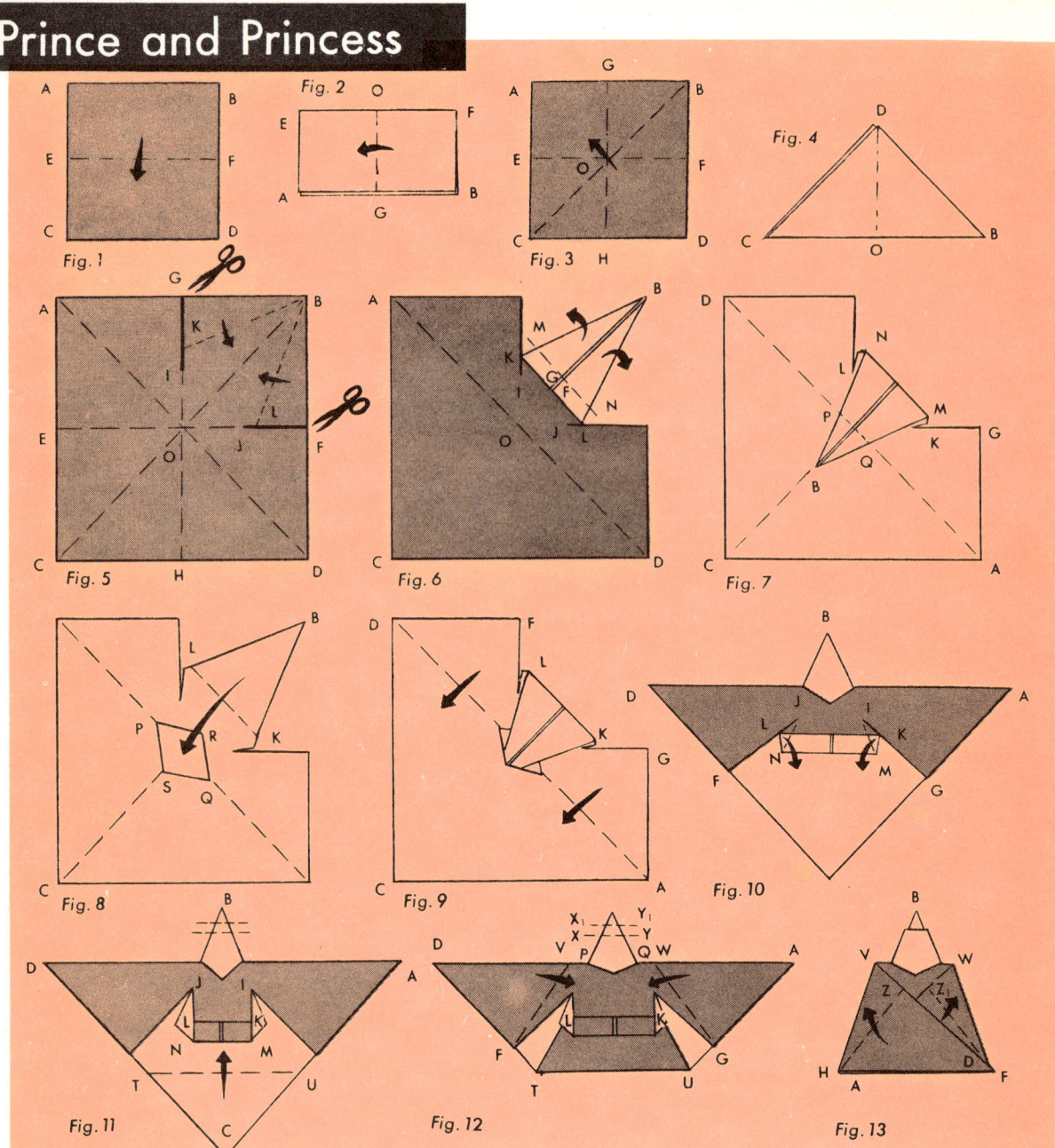

1. To make the "Prince," fold a square sheet of paper along line EF (FIG. 1) so that AB falls on CD (FIG. 2).
2. Fold along OG (FIG. 2) so that FB falls on EA; then open (FIG. 3).
3. Fold along CB (FIG. 3) so that D falls on A (FIG. 4).
4. Fold along DO so that B falls on C (FIG. 4); then open (FIG. 5).
5. Cut along GI and FJ, each cut being a little less than two-thirds of the way towards the center O (FIG. 5).
6. Fold along KB and LB so that GB meets BF at center BO (FIGS. 5 & 6).
7. Fold back along MN (FIG. 6) and turn the paper over so that B falls on OC (FIG. 7). MN is less than two-thirds of the way down BO.
8. Mark PQ along DA (FIG. 7) and cut out diamond shape PRQS, R and S being on BC (FIG. 8).
9. Bring point B forward through opening PRQS (FIG. 9).
10. Fold along DA (FIG. 9), bringing F and G forward, and point B will come up by itself (FIG. 10).
11. Fold along JN and IM (FIG. 10), opening L and K (FIG. 11).
12. Fold along TU (FIG. 11), putting C under the front body flap (FIG. 12).
13. Fold along VF and WG (FIG. 12), bringing points D and A forward, V and W being nearly ½ inch from P and Q, respectively (FIG. 13).

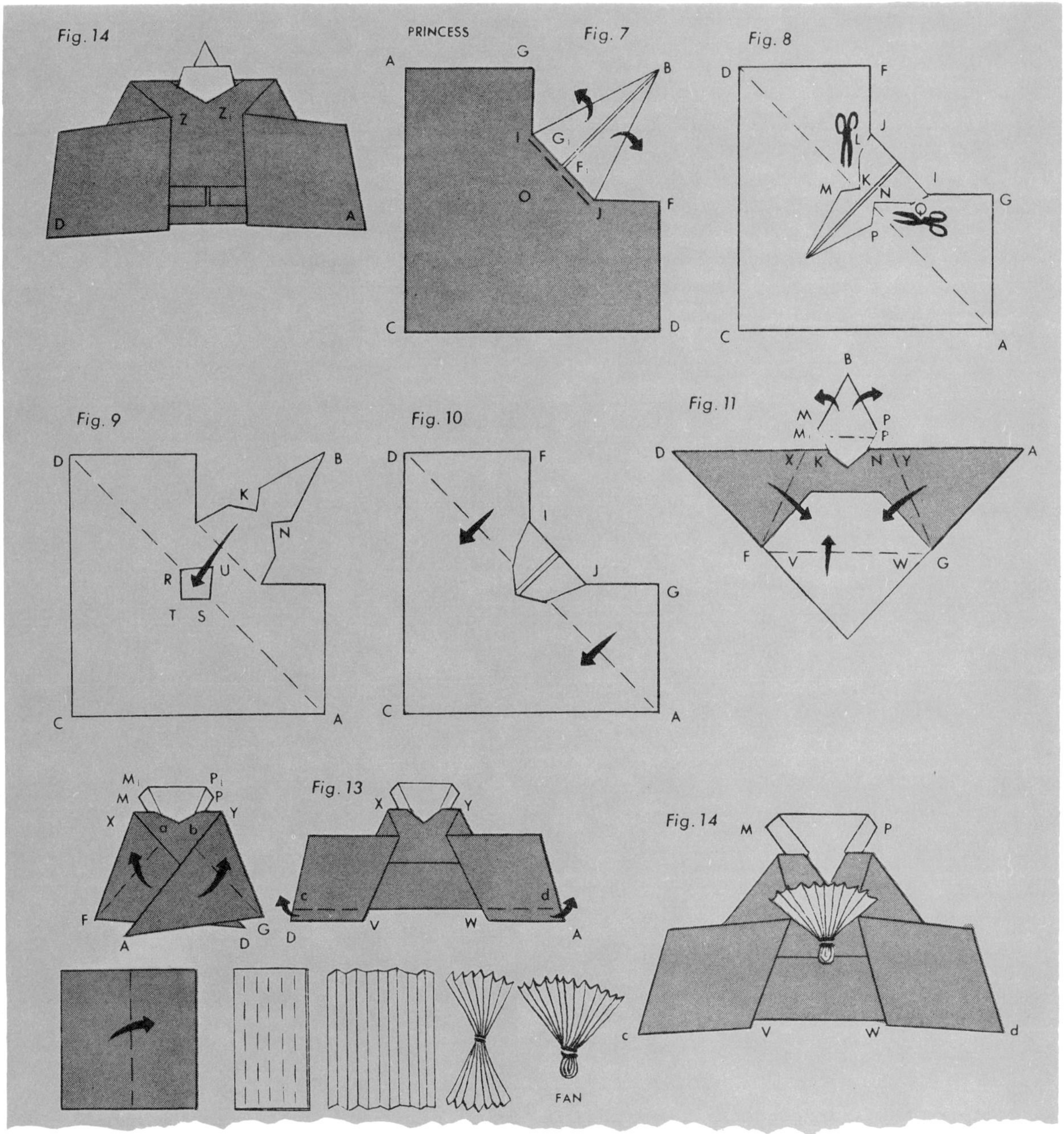

Fig. 14

PRINCESS Fig. 7

Fig. 8

Fig. 9

Fig. 10

Fig. 11

Fig. 13

Fig. 14

FAN

14. Make the head piece by folding along XY, bringing point B back along OC (FIG. 12), then again at X_1Y_1, bringing B up (FIG. 13).

15. Fold along ZH (FIG. 13), opening corner D so that DZ falls on HZ. Do the same for A, folding along Z_1F (FIG. 14).

To MAKE THE "PRINCESS," repeat steps 1 through 6 of "Prince" (Figs. 1–6) and follow the diagrams closely from Fig. 7 on. The main difference is in the cutting of the notches to make the head piece.

With another piece of paper, make a pleated paper fan for the princess. See *Origami: Book One*, p. 8, "Fan."

Motorboat

1. Fold a square piece of paper along EG, GF, FH, HE so that corners A, B, C, D will all meet at center point O (FIGS. 1 & 2).
2. Fold along IJ, KL, MN, and PQ (FIG. 2) so that corners A and D are inside the flap (FIG. 3) touching edges EG and HF, respectively, while corners C and B touch edges EH and GF from the outside (FIG. 3).
3. Turn over; fold along RS and VW (FIG. 4) so that edges GE and FH meet at center TU (FIG. 5).
4. Fold corners R, S, V, and W forward (FIG. 5) so that RT, SU, TV, and UW fall on TU (FIG. 6).
5. Fold along TX, XU, UY and TY (FIG. 6), bringing corners a, b, c, and d forward (FIG. 7). Points x and y are centers of ab and cd, respectively.

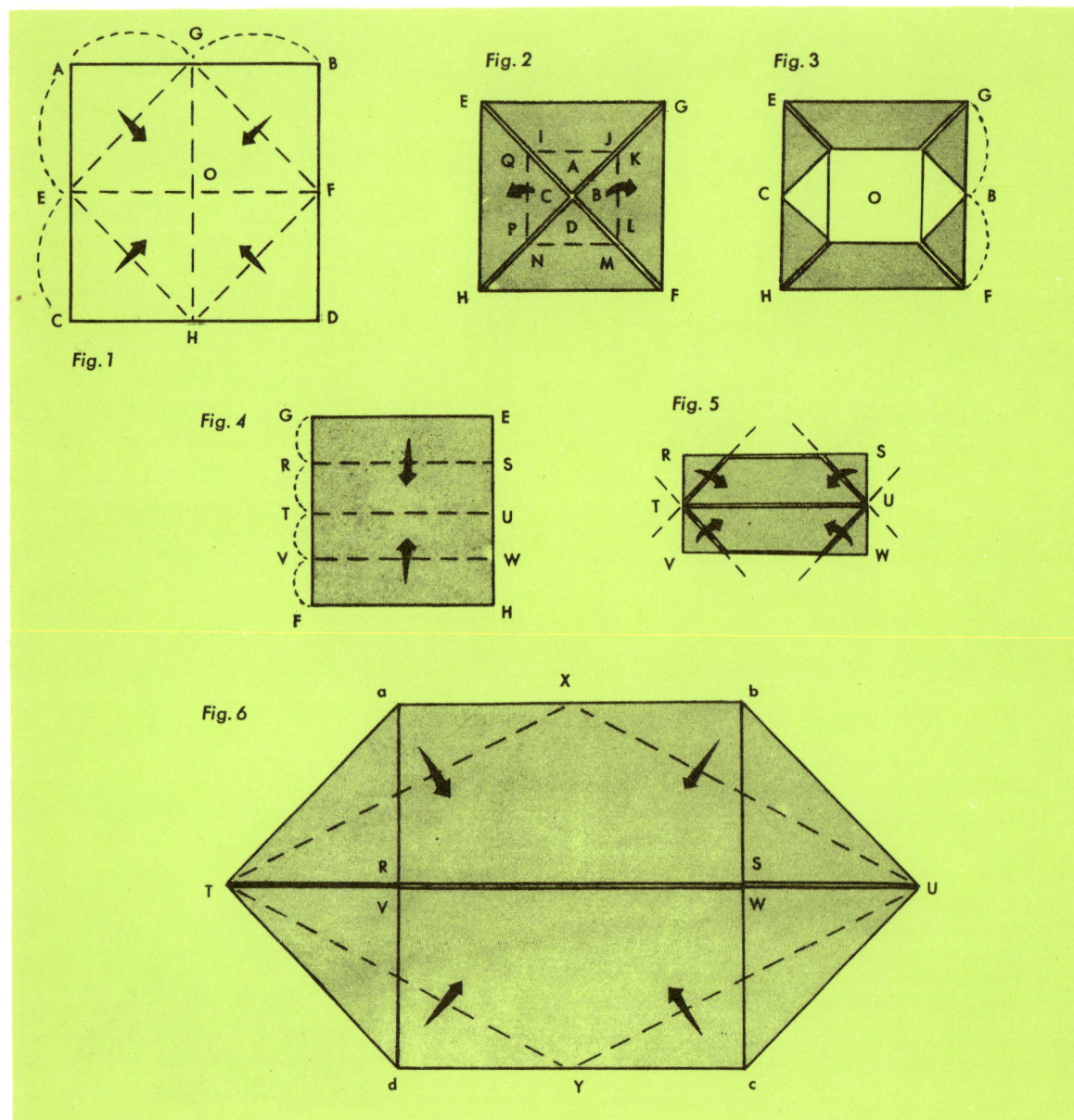

6. Fold along ef and gh (FIG. 7), bringing corners x and y forward (FIG. 8).
7. Fold out in half along TU (FIGS. 8 & 9).
8. Take the two outer flaps (FIG. 9), one in each hand, and turn the entire object inside out (FIG. 10).
   See *Origami: Book Two*, p. 25, "Rowboat," Figs. 3–8.

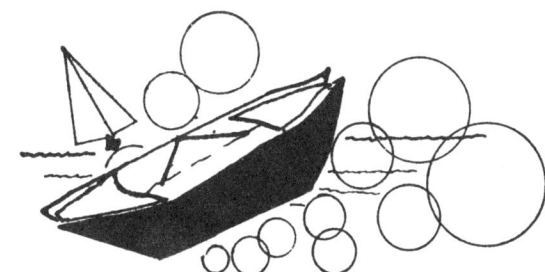

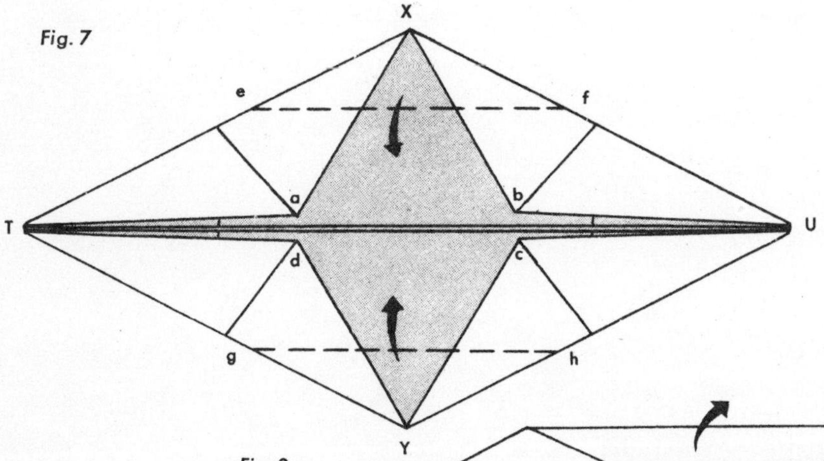

Fig. 7

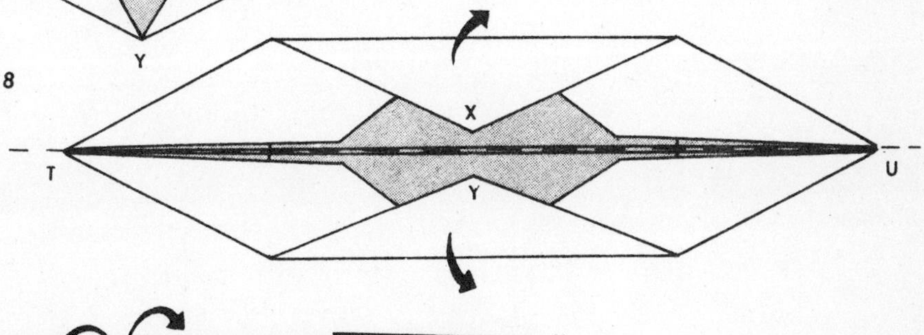

Fig. 8

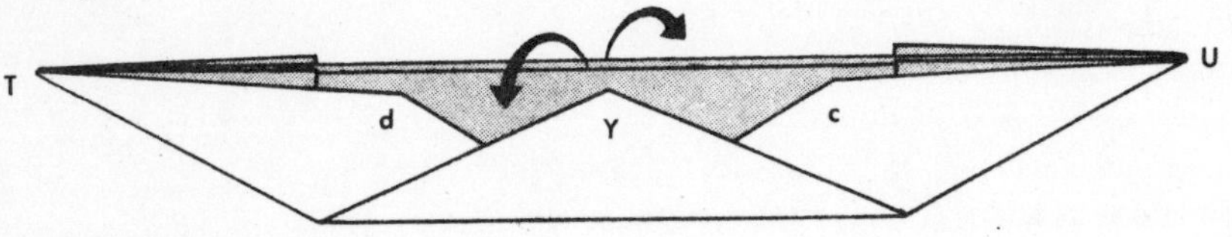

Fig. 9

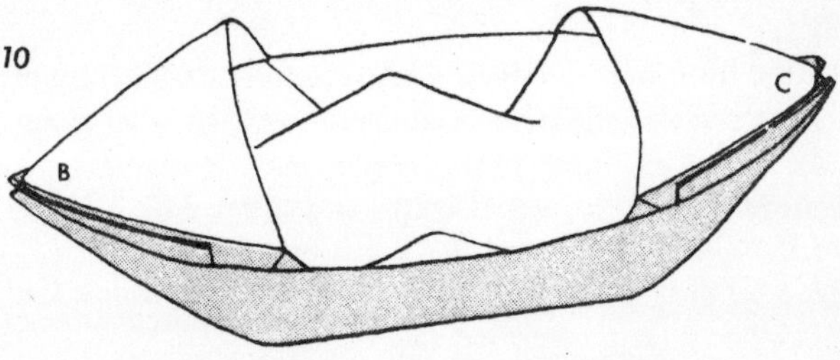

Fig. 10

Pig

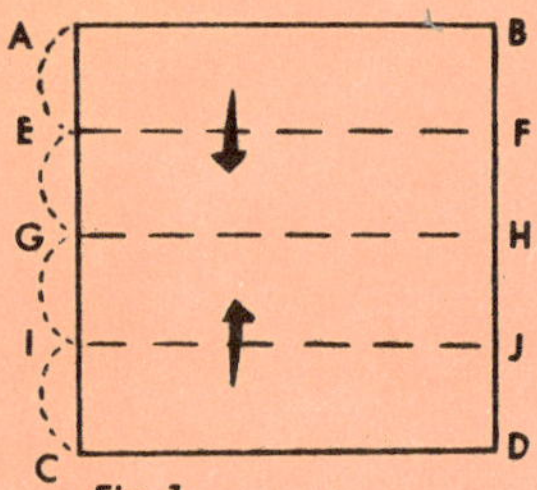

Fig. 1

Fig. 2
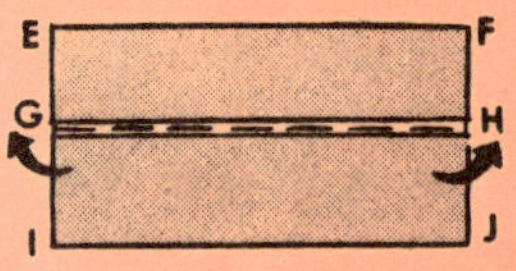

Fig. 3
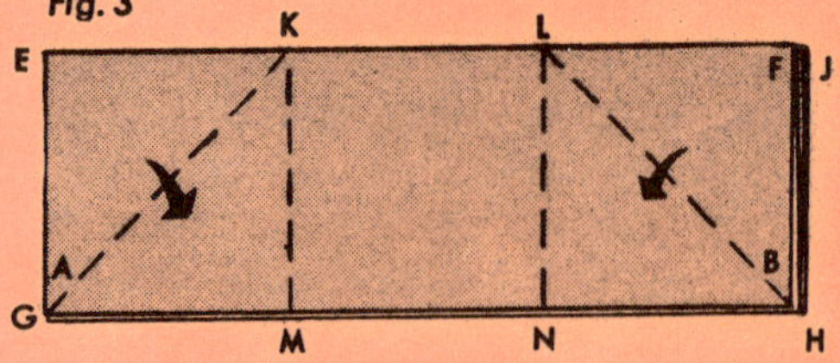

Fig. 4
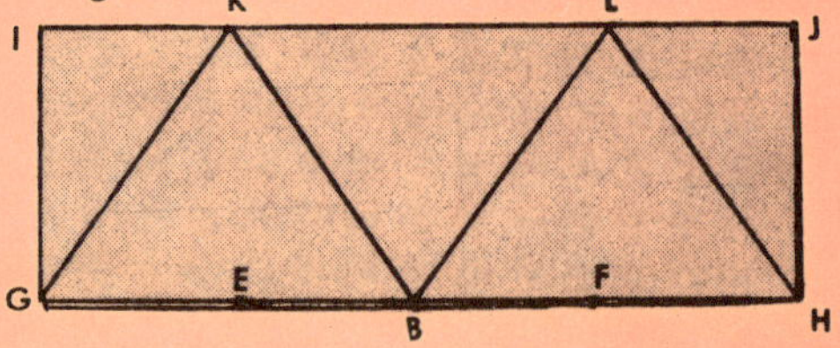

Fig. 5
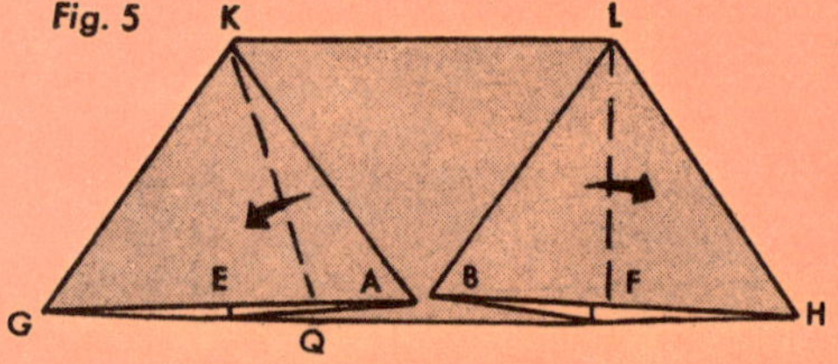

Fig. 6
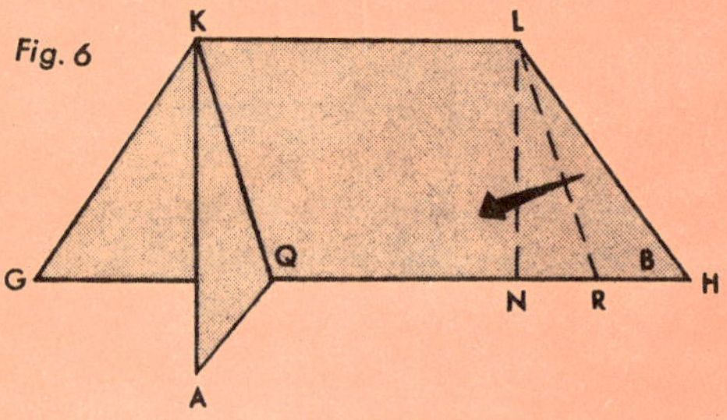

Fig. 7
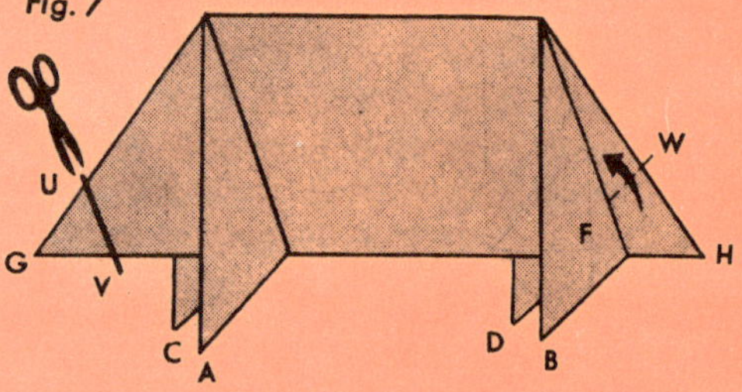

Fig. 8
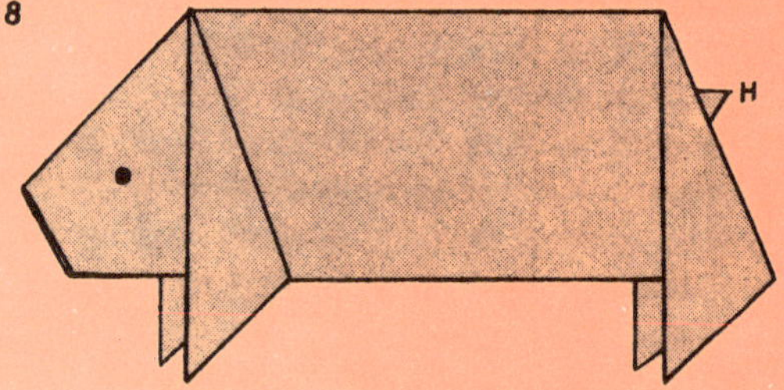

1. Fold a square piece of paper along EF and IJ (FIG. 1) so that edges AB and CD meet at center GH (FIG. 2).
2. Fold in half along GH (FIG. 2) so that IJ falls on the back side of EF (FIG. 3).
3. Take the front flap and open corners E and F (FIG. 3) by bringing A to the right and B to the left so that they meet each other along HG. EK falls on MK and FL on NL, respectively (FIG. 4).
4. Turn over and repeat step 3 with I and J (FIG. 5).
5. Fold along KQ (FIG. 5) so that KA falls on KE (FIG. 6).
6. Move B to the right (FIG. 5) so that edge LB falls on LH (FIG. 6).
7. Fold along LR (FIG. 6) so that LH falls on LN.
8. Turn over and repeat steps 5, 6, and 7 (FIG. 7).
9. Cut off point G at UV and draw dots for the eyes (FIGS. 7 & 8).
10. To make the tail, fold along WF (FIG. 7) and push H in between the body flaps (FIG. 8).

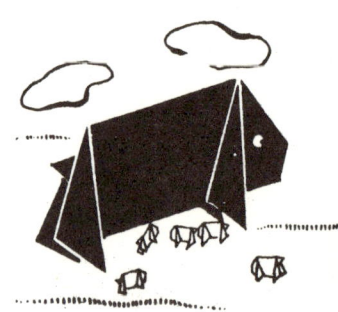

Chair

1. Fold a square piece of paper along EF (FIG. 1) so that AB falls on CD (FIG. 2).
2. Fold along GH so that FB falls on EA (FIG. 2). Fold again in half; then open (FIG. 3).
3. Fold forward along YM and NZ (FIG. 4) so that EM and NF fall on MO and NP, respectively. Then open. M and N are halfway between IG and GK.
4. Fold along IJ and KL so that the two edges fall on center GH (FIGS. 4 & 5).
5. Fold back along QSR and open (FIG. 5).
6. Open corner K so that SR falls on top of SL (FIGS. 5, 6, 7).
7. Repeat step 6 with corner I (FIG. 8).
8. By lifting the top flaps at EQRF, crease along IO and KP (FIG. 8) so that AO and PB form right angles to OJ and LP, respectively (FIGS. 9 and 10).

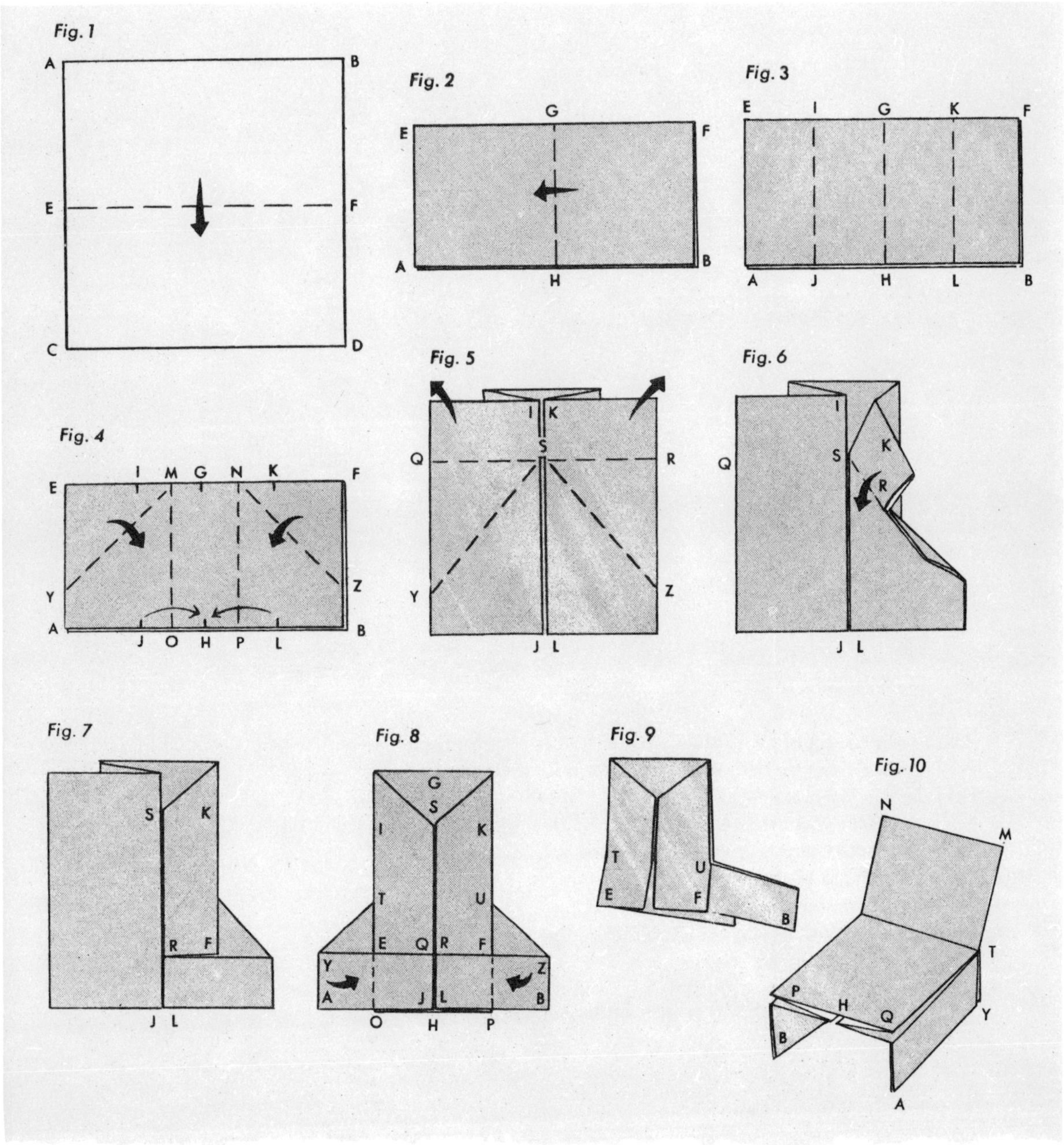

Table

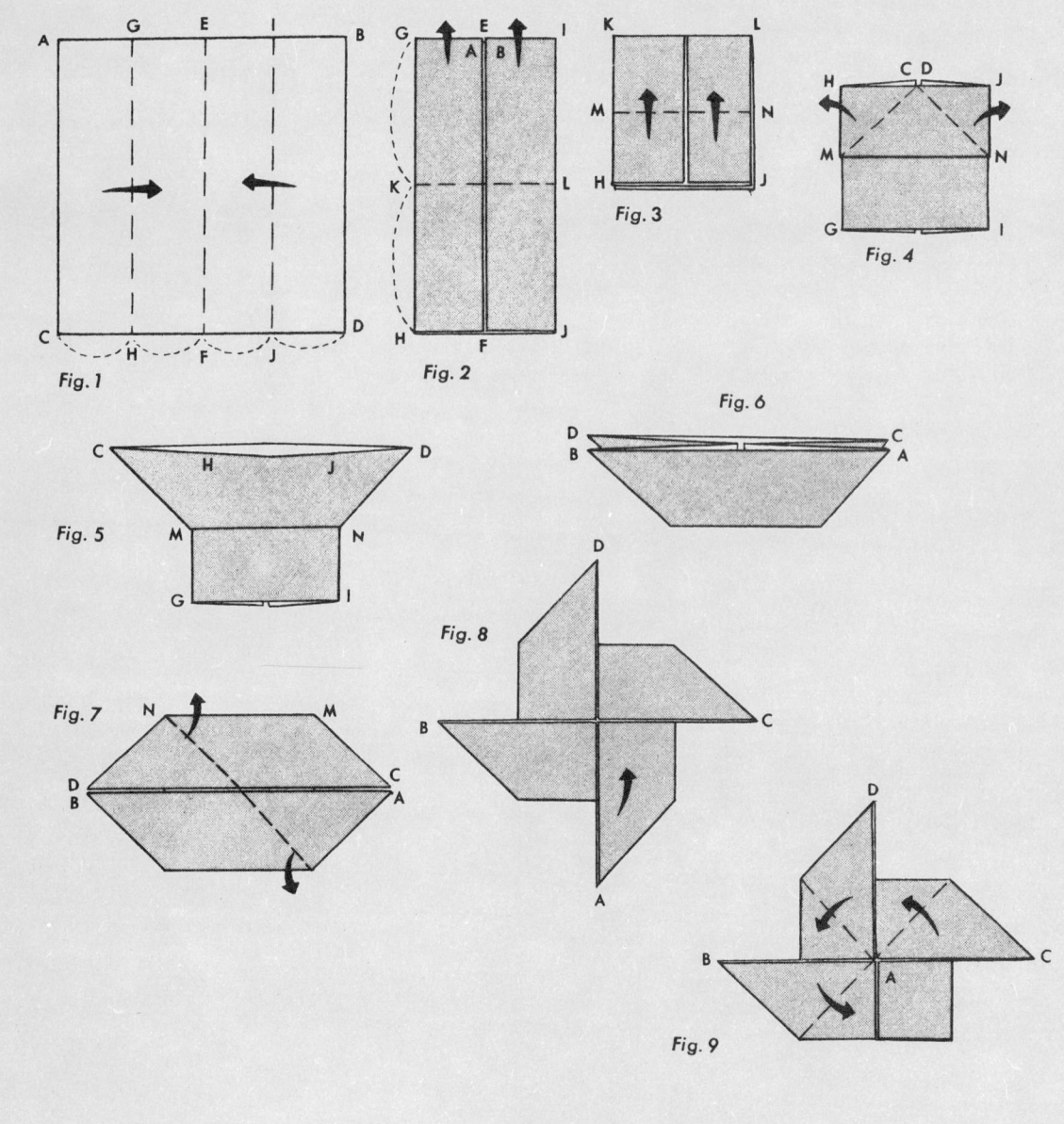

1. Fold a square piece of paper along GH and IJ (FIG. 1) so that edges AC and BD meet at center EF (FIG. 2).
2. Fold GI back along KL (FIG. 2) so that GI will be under HJ (FIG. 3).
3. Fold the top flap along MN (FIG. 3) so that HJ falls on KL (FIG. 4).
4. Make a crease along CM and DN (FIG. 4) and then pull out corners C and D (FIG. 5).
5. Turn the paper over and repeat steps 3 and 4.
6. Spread out FIG. 6 so that it looks like FIG. 7.
7. Fold D upward and A downward (FIGS. 7 & 8).
8. Open corner A (FIG. 8) and bring point A to the center (FIG. 9).*
9. Repeat step 8 at B, C, and D (FIGS. 9 & 10).
10. Crease at OD and PD (FIG. 10) so that QD and JD meet at center. Then crease at OP. Lift up D, folding along OP so that Q and J meet at the middle (FIG. 11) on DZ.**

Fig. 10 Fig. 11 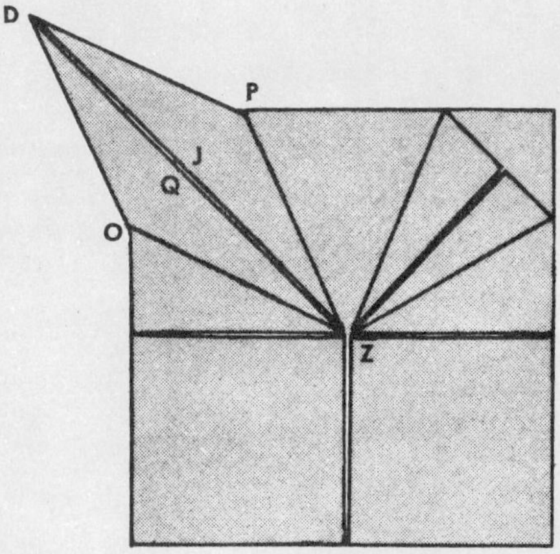 Fig. 12 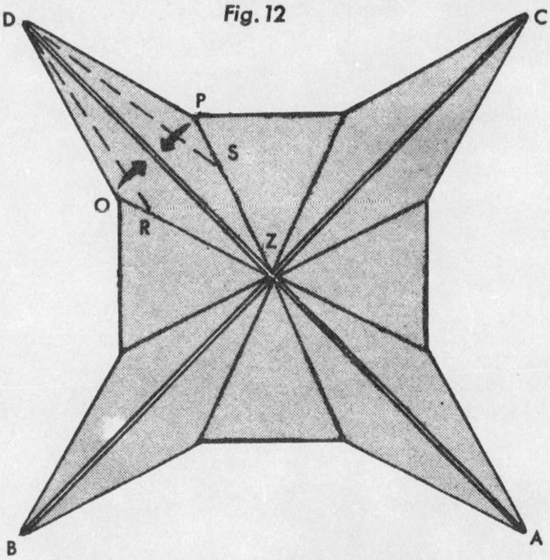 Fig. 13 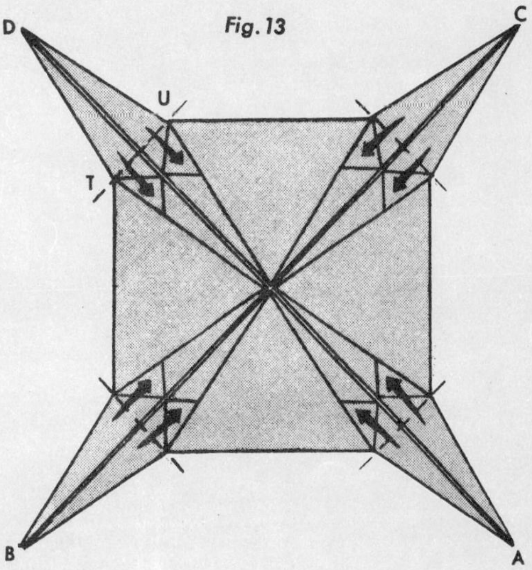 Fig. 14

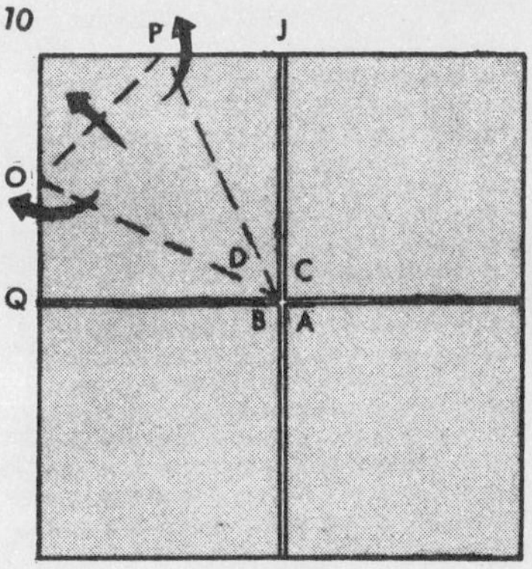

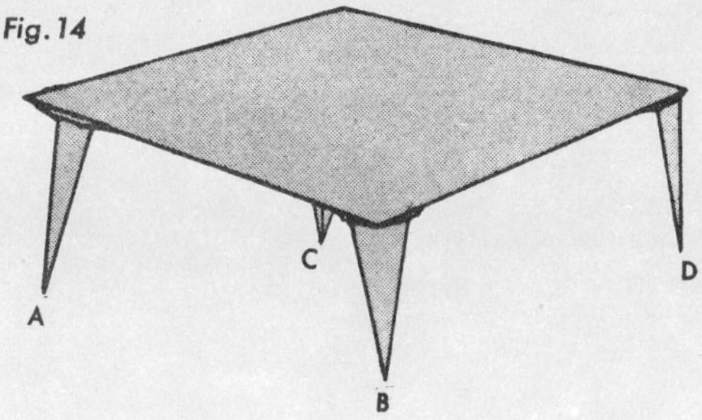

11. Repeat step 10 for other corners A, B, and C (FIGS. 11 & 12).
12. Fold along DR and DS (FIG. 12) so that DO meets DP at center on DZ.
13. Repeat step 12 on A, B, and C (FIG. 13).
14. To make the legs stand, fold along TU (FIG. 13).
15. Repeat step 14 on C, A, and B (FIG. 14).
   * See *Origami: Book One*, p. 26, "Windmill," Figs. 1–9, or *Origami: Book Two*, p. 28, "Flower," Figs. 1–9.
   ** See *Origami: Book Two*, p. 22, "Robin," Figs. 6–8.

23

Space Ship

1. Fold a square piece of paper along GH and IJ (FIG. 1) so that AC and BD meet at center EF (FIG. 2).
2. Fold GI back along KL (FIG. 2) so that GI will be under HJ (FIG. 3).
3. Fold along MN (FIG. 3) so that HJ falls on KL (FIG. 4).
4. Crease along CM and DN (FIG. 4) and then pull out corners C and D, thus opening H and J (FIG. 5). Turn over and repeat steps 3 and 4.
5. Spread out FIG. 6 so that it looks like FIG. 7.
6. Turn paper over (FIG. 8). Fold along QR so that OP falls on BA (FIG. 9).
7. Fold along center (FIG. 9) so that DC falls on BA (FIG. 10).
8. Fold along ST (FIG. 10) so that SM falls on SF (FIG. 11).
9. Repeat step 9 with SJ (FIGS. 11 & 12).
10. Turn over (FIG. 13). Fold along VW and XY so that they meet (FIG. 14).

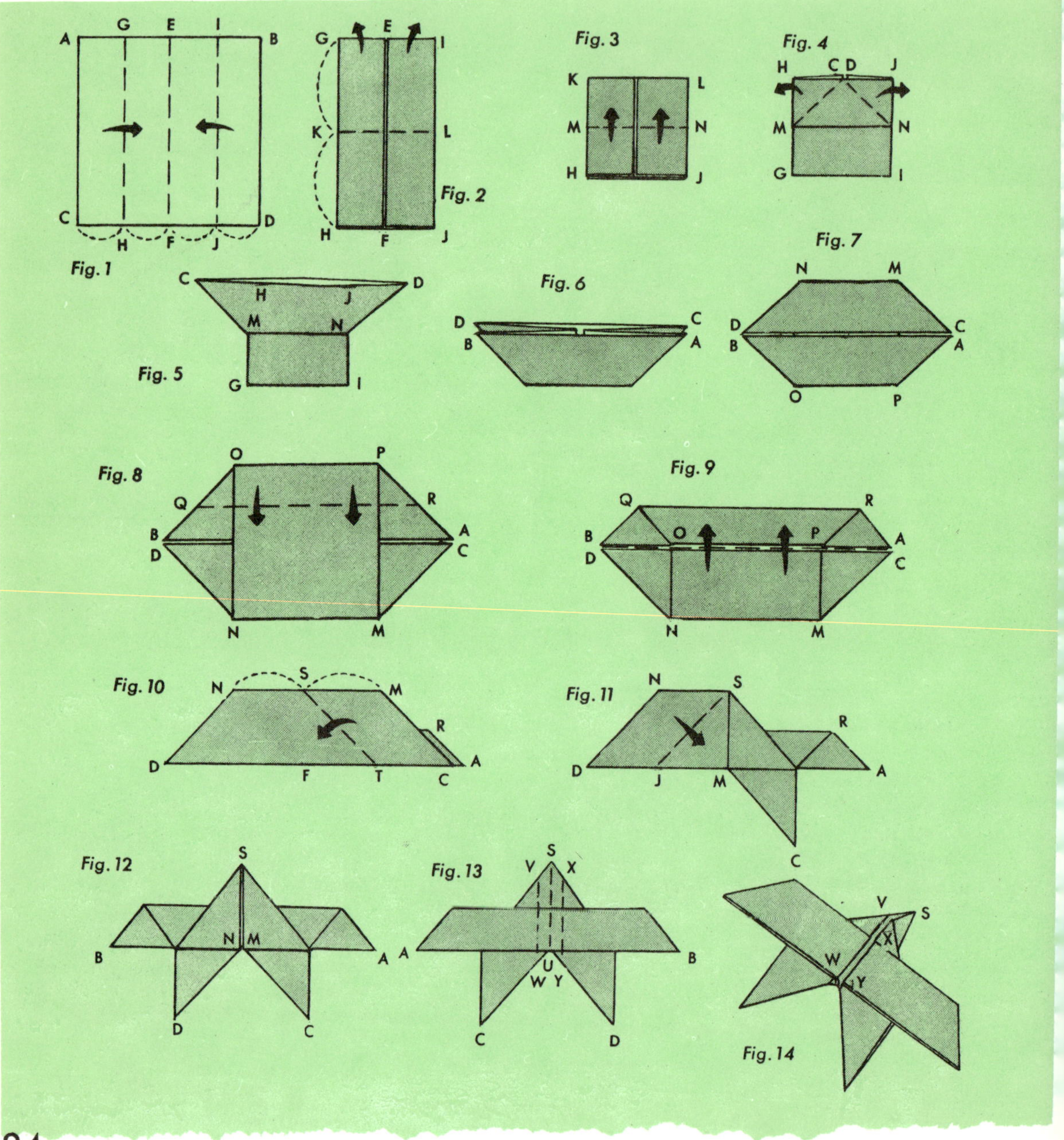

24

Treasure Box

Fig. 1   *Fig. 2*   *Fig. 3*   *Fig. 4*   *Fig. 5*   *Fig. 6*   *Fig. 7*

1. Fold a square piece of paper along EH, HF, GF, and EG (FIGS. 1 & 2) so that corners A, B, C, and D meet at center O (FIG. 3). E, F, G, and H are center points of each edge.
2. Crease along IJ, KL, MN, OP (FIG. 3), each crease being just a little less than halfway in towards the center.
3. Open out corners A and D as in Fig. 4.
4. Fold along MN and OP (FIG. 4) and push in corners H and F so that LR meets RN and TK meets TP (FIG. 5).
5. Fold along LK so that NP falls on RT and corner D meets B and C at center (FIG. 5).
6. Repeat steps 4 and 5 with corners E, G, and A (FIG. 6).

    By using square papers of different sizes you can get one box to fit over the other like a lid or make a nest of boxes of all sizes, one inside the other.

25

Penguin

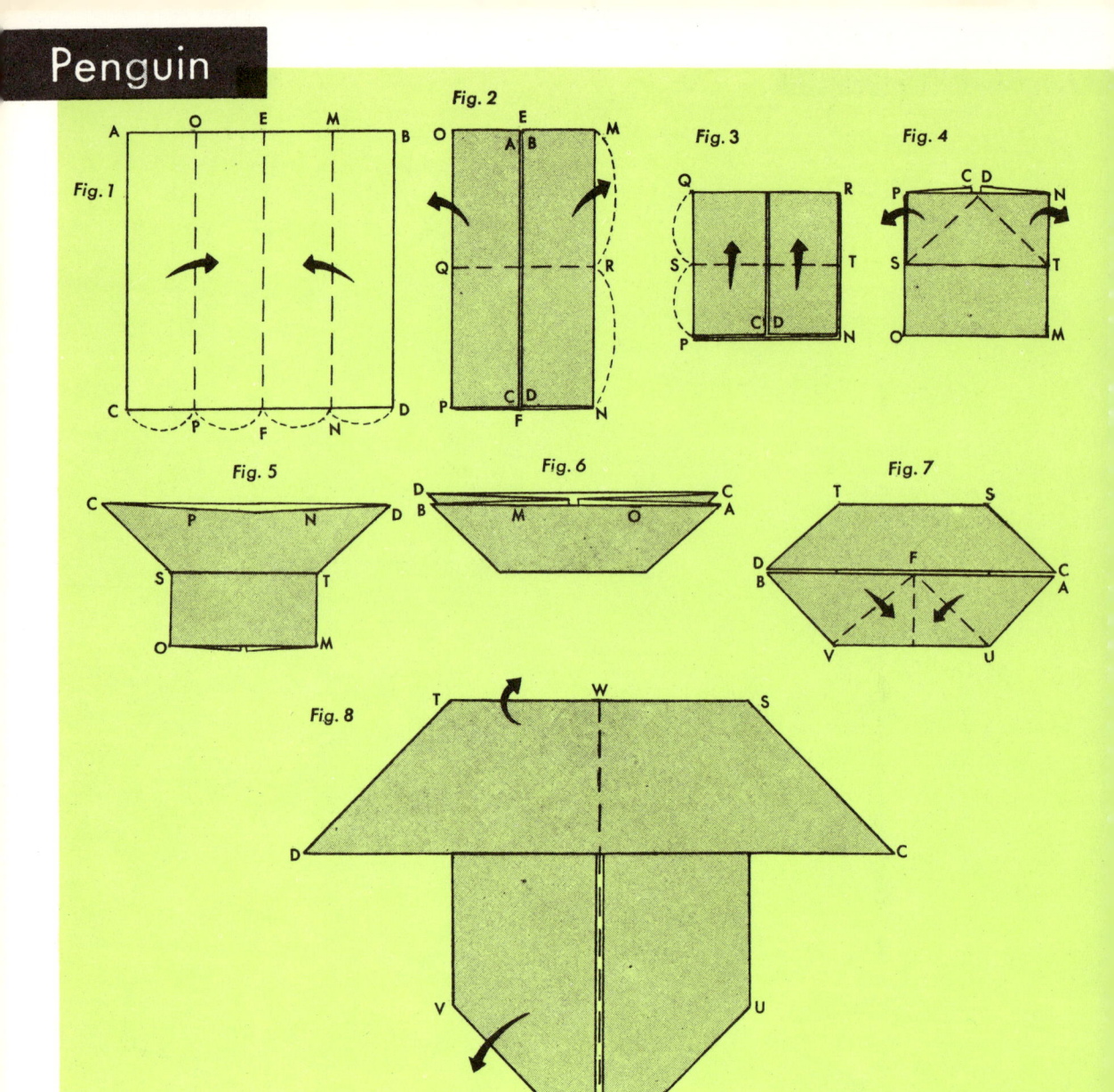

1. Fold a square piece of paper along lines OP and MN (FIG. 1) so that edges AC and BD meet at the center EF (FIG. 2).
2. Fold OM back along QR (FIG. 2) so that OM will be under PN (FIG. 3).
3. Fold along ST (FIG. 3) so that PN falls on QR (FIG. 4).
4. Make a crease along CS and DT (FIG. 4) and then pull out corners C and D (FIG. 5).
5. Turn the paper over and repeat steps 3 and 4 (FIG. 6).
6. Spread out Fig. 6 so that it looks like Fig. 7.
7. Fold along FV and FU, bringing B and A downward to meet at center (FIGS. 7 & 8).
8. Fold in half along WA so that S and T, C and D, U and V meet respectively (FIG. 9).

26

Fig. 9 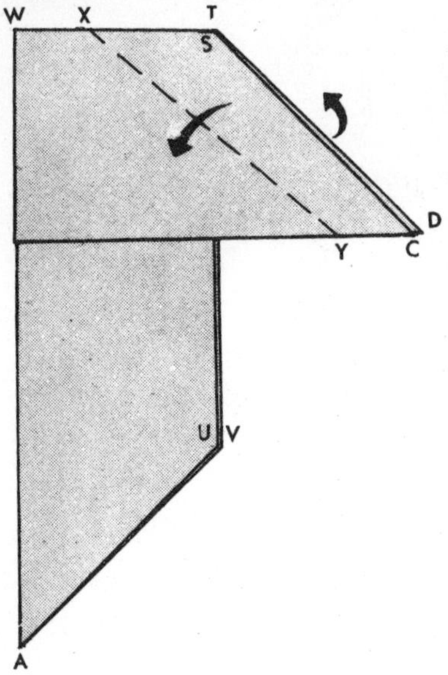
Fig. 10 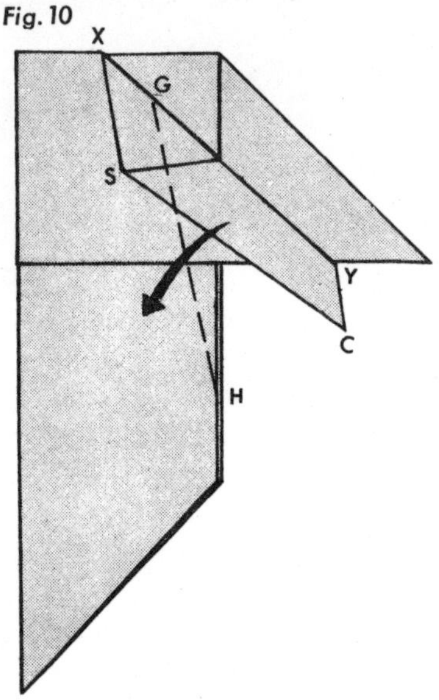
Fig. 11 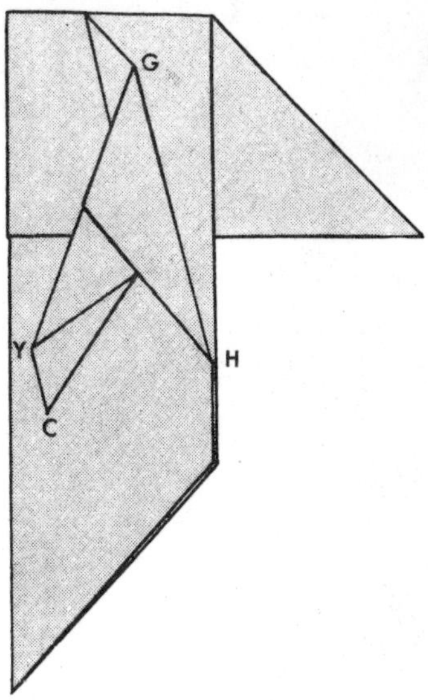
Fig. 12 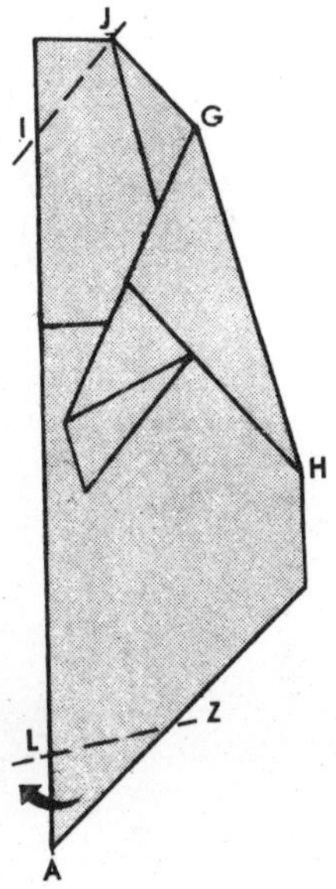
Fig. 13 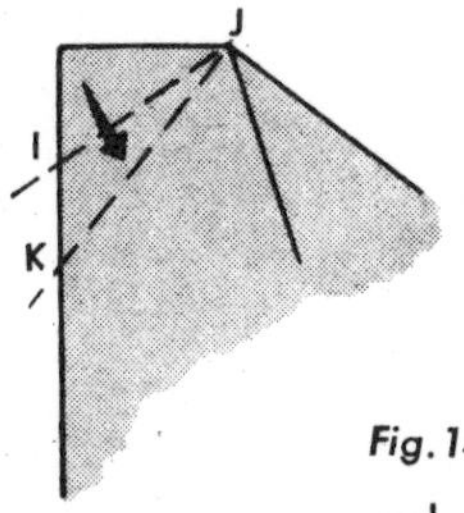
Fig. 14 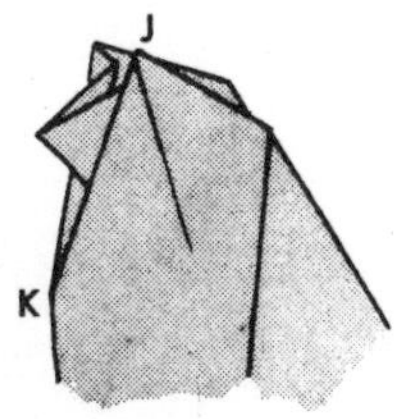
Fig. 15

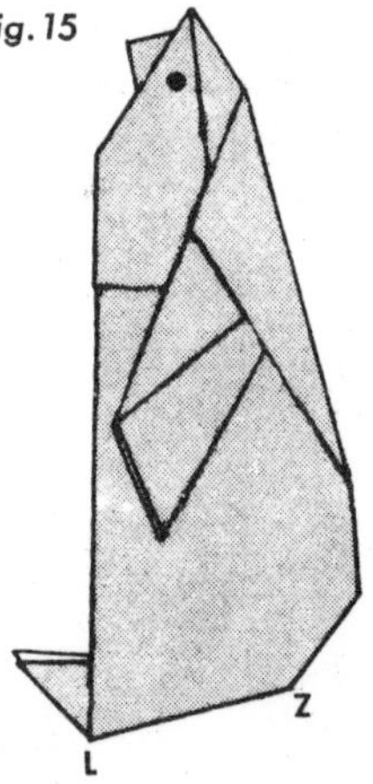

9. Fold along XY, bringing S and C in front (FIG. 9 & 10).
10. Fold again at GH, bringing YC forward (FIG. 11).
11. Repeat steps 9 and 10 on other side of body flap (FIG. 12).
12. To make the head, fold along IJ and KJ (FIG. 13) pushing IJ back in between the body flaps (FIG. 14).
13. To make the feet, fold along LZ (FIG. 12), putting A in between body flaps.
14. Do the same on the other side (FIG. 15).

PARTY

Applications of Origami

In the following pages you will find different ways of using *origami* objects which you have thus far folded. Here are some party suggestions. These figures are all from *Origami: Book One, Two,* and *Three*. See if you can think of other ways to use these paper creations.

(1) Lantern, *Bk. 1*, p. 22
(2) Clown, *Bk. 2*, p. 13
(3) Fish, *Bk. 1*, p. 24
(4) Flowers, *Bk. 1*, p. 14
(5) Flower, *Bk. 2*, p. 28
(6) Candy Box, *Bk. 2*, p. 30
(7) Treasure Box, *Bk. 3*, p. 25
(8) Rabbit, *Bk. 2*, p. 18
(9) Swan, *Bk. 1*, p. 28
(10) Crane, *Bk. 1*, p. 30
(11) Wolf, *Bk. 2*, p. 6
(12) Caps, *Bk. 3*, p. 7
(13) Cat, *Bk. 2*, p. 9
(14) Helmet, *Bk. 1*, p. 18
(15) Dog, *Bk. 2*, p. 8
(16) Robin, *Bk. 2*, p. 22
(17) Santa Claus, *Bk. 1*, p. 10
(18) Kimono, *Bk. 2*, p. 16

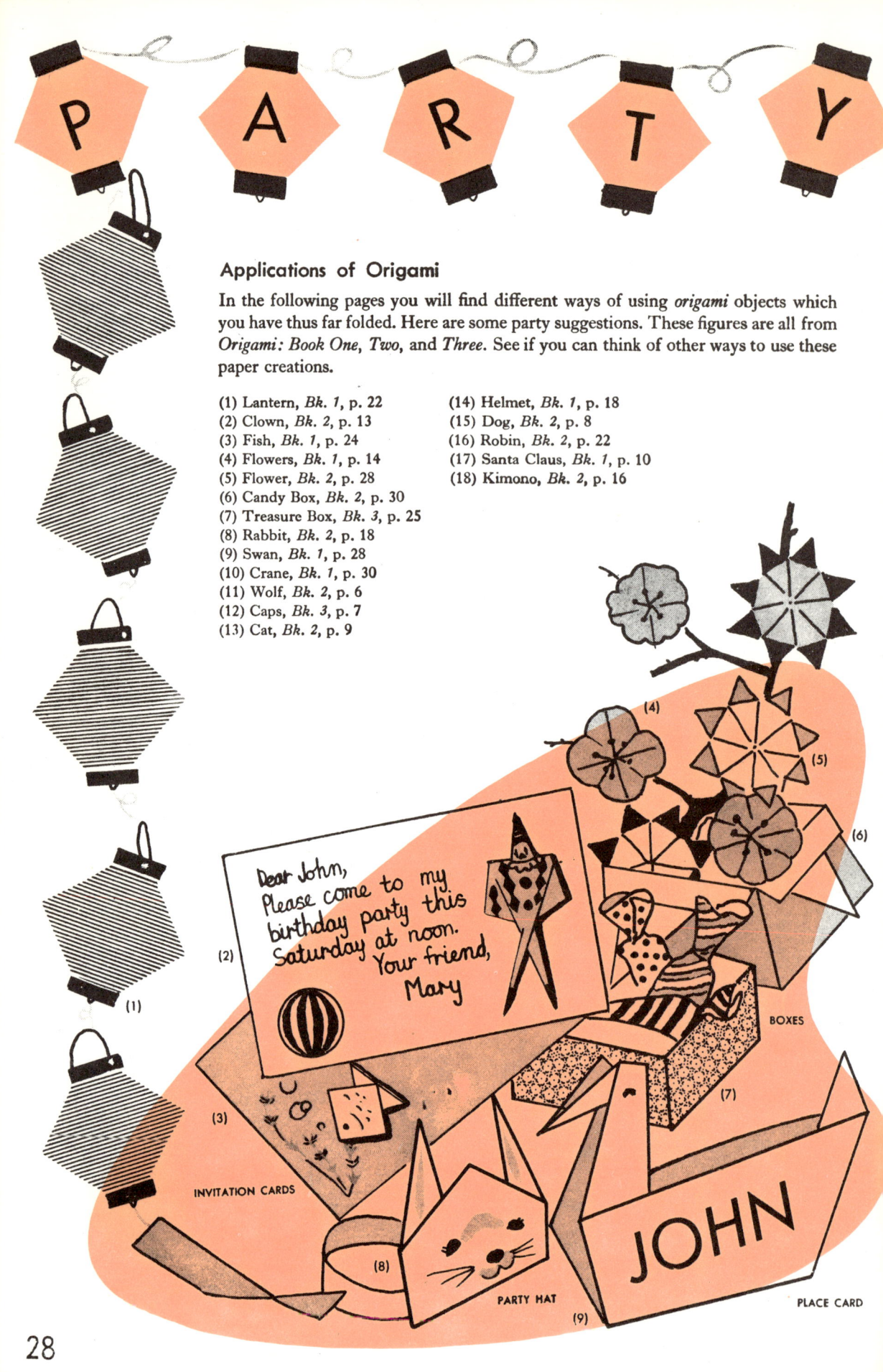

Boat Race

Make boats of various sizes and colors. Tie one end of a piece of string to each boat and the other end to the middle of a pencil. At the starting signal each player winds the string on his pencil, thus pulling his boat towards him. The first boat reaching the goal wins the race.
(1) Motorboat, *Bk. 3*, p. 18   (2) Rowboat, *Bk. 2*, p. 25

Mobile

By stringing various *origami* objects of different sizes and colors make a mobile with wires. As shown in the above picture, the objects need not be restricted to things that fly.

Space Travel

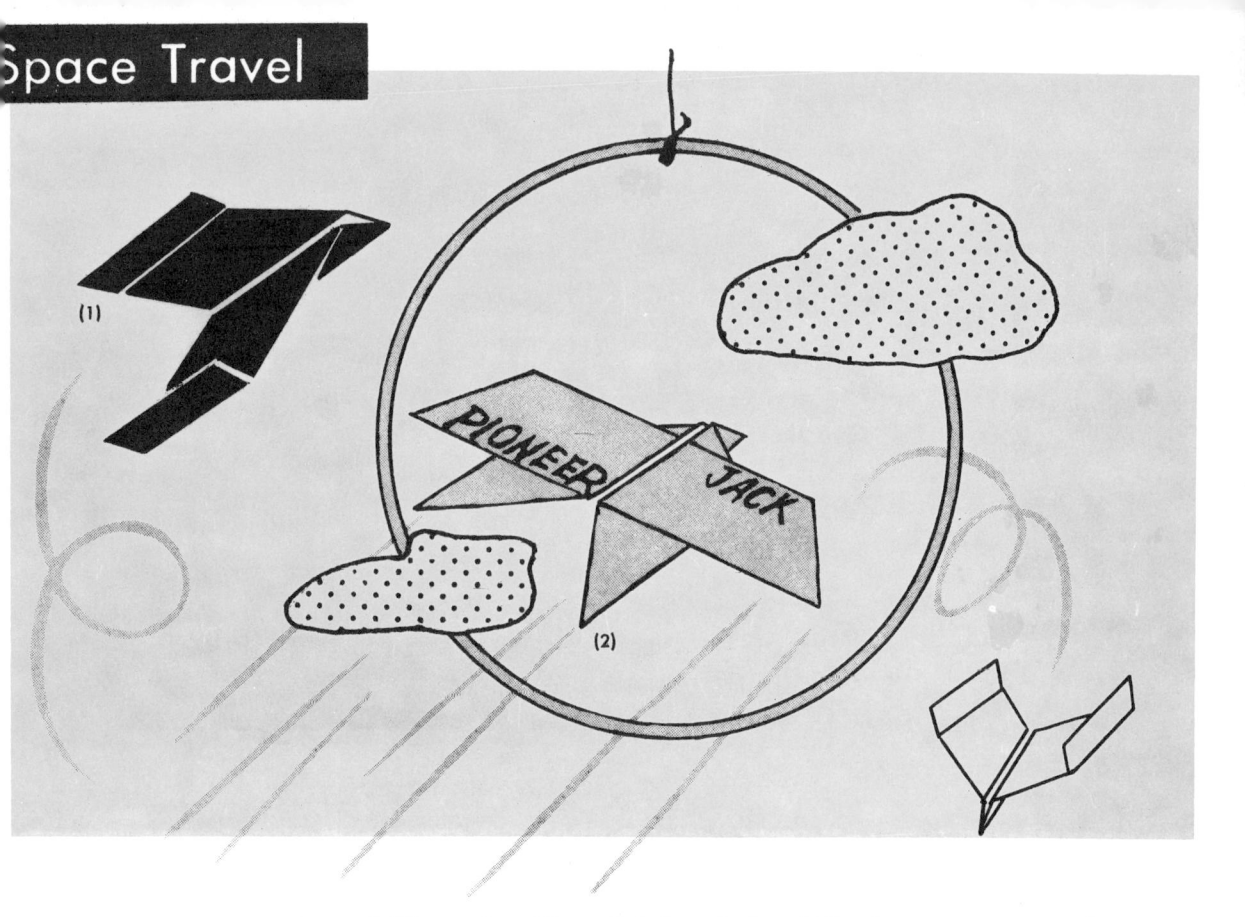

Use space ships and jet planes of different sizes. Hang a hula hoop in the middle of a room to represent the moon. Attach pieces of paper clouds for obstacles as in the picture. Stand at a distance and fly your planes through the clouds to the "moon." See whose plane gets there first. This game can be played both indoors and out.   (1) Jet Plane, *Bk. 3*, p. 13   (2) Space Ship, *Bk. 3*, p. 24

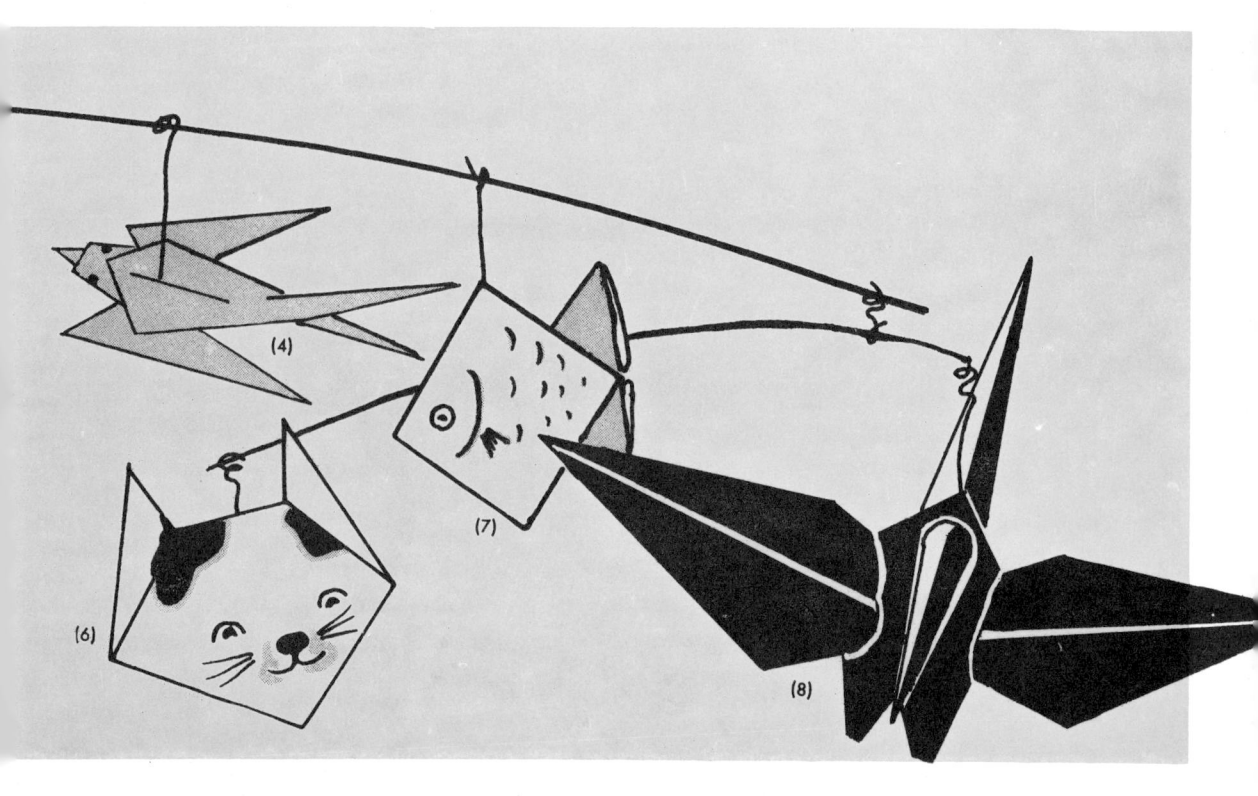

(1) Peacock, *Bk. 2*, p. 10   (3) Bird, *Bk. 3*, p. 9   (5) Space Ship, *Bk. 3*, p. 24   (7) Fish, *Bk. 1*, p. 24
(2) Robin, *Bk. 2*, p. 22   (4) Swallow, *Bk. 3*, p. 10   (6) Cat, *Bk. 2*, p. 9   (8) Crane, *Bk. 1*, p. 30

31

Hunting Game

Arrange various *origami* objects on a table. Put point marks on each object as shown above. Stand at a distance from the table and, with a rubber band as a slingshot, shoot these objects and let them fall. The one who gets the most points is the best hunter. Besides this hunting game, you can also make a miniature zoo with the different animals in *Books One*, *Two*, and *Three*.

(1) Penguin, *Bk. 3*, p. 26
(2) Whale, *Bk. 3*, p. 8
(3) Giraffe, *Bk. 2*, p. 12
(4) Peahen, *Bk. 2*, p. 11
(5) Pig, *Bk. 3*, p. 20
(6) Tree, *Bk. 1*, p. 12
(7) Elephant, *Bk. 2*, p. 14
(8) Rabbit, *Bk. 2*, p. 18
(9) Tent, *Bk. 3*, p. 12
(10) Wolf, *Bk. 2*, p. 6